IF I KNEW THEN WHAT I KNOW NOW...

A RUNNER'S HANDBOOK

Gavin Spickett

IF I KNEW THEN | WHAT I KNOW NOW....

A RUNNER'S HANDBOOK

 THE CROWOOD PRESS

First published in 2023 by
The Crowood Press Ltd
Ramsbury, Marlborough
Wiltshire SN8 2HR

enquiries@crowood.com
www.crowood.com

British Library Cataloguing-in-Publication Data
A catalogue record for this book is available from the British Library.

ISBN 978 0 7198 4291 7

Cover design by Sergey Tsvetkov
Frontispiece: Finlay Wild in the 2015 Ben Nevis Race. (Photo: Paul Dobson/Wikimedia Commons)

Disclaimer
This book is based on the author's knowledge and personal experience. Information has been checked carefully. This book is not a substitute for taking personal professional advice, especially in regard to illness or injury and the information therein is supplied without liability. The Author and Publisher will not be liable for any possible disadvantage, injury or damages.

Typeset by Simon and Sons
Printed and bound in India by Thomson Press India Ltd

CONTENTS

PREFACE

The author competing in the Lakeland Trails Hellvellyn Challenge.
Reproduced with permission from Lakeland Trails, photographed by Carlos Reina.

Why have I come to write this book? I am not a famous runner, I have not achieved fastest known times, represented my country or indeed been anything other than a well-established local runner, doing road races, trail races and ultra-events. I have been running now for over 25 years. I have recently retired as a consultant after 41 years in the NHS and 30 years working as a consultant in the North East, dealing with allergy and immunology. I have also been involved in setting up running the regional service for chronic fatigue syndrome (ME) and

have become involved with athletes who have developed the overtraining syndrome. I have been directly involved in sports medicine and I've latterly qualified as a fitness instructor. I'm a member of my local running club as well as professional bodies for strength and conditioning trainers and fitness professionals.

I have run and trained pretty consistently over the last 25 years and along the way I have picked up lots of useful information. A lot of this was not available to me when I started off on my running journey. As a doctor and a research scientist, I am always evaluating information rather than blindly accepting it. My opinions may therefore diverge from orthodoxy and I make no apology for this! Reading published information can be extremely confusing, especially for new runners, with completely contradictory advice available. Even supposedly simple books can have a lot of confusing and complicated science, none of which is really relevant to day-to-day running. How do you choose what is best? I hope that this book will add some clarity.

When I started running equipment was simpler, the choice of shoes and clothing was simpler, GPS watches had not been invented and for average club runners, advice on training and preparation was fairly limited. Shoes, clothing and other equipment have improved beyond recognition and the latest generation of sports watches can, if used correctly, provide valuable insights into training. However, the bottom line remains that running in its simplest form is exercise which can be done with fairly basic shoes and clothing and for the majority of people setting out on their running journey, expensive fancy equipment is unnecessary.

Thirty years ago, apart from large events such as the London Marathon and the Great North Run, most running events were directly organised by the running clubs themselves. The workload of dealing with the police, local councils, private landowners, obtaining first-aid cover and arranging insurance has meant that many of the running clubs have ceased to organise events and most are coordinated by specific event management companies. This development has had a positive benefit in the quality of support, from the moment of booking a place to the end of the event.

Nonetheless on race day, all the events are still dependent on the time and dedication of volunteers to man marshalling points, registration and the finish line. These volunteers give up their time so that runners can undertake their hobby: it is important the participants should always thank volunteers and the organisers. Be courteous to marshals. Without the volunteers, many events would not be allowed to take place. Be prepared to volunteer yourself.

This book is primarily for adults starting out on their running journey or who have reached a point where they are looking towards new and different challenges. However, established runners can skip the 'how to begin' chapters and move on to how to progress. This book is not necessarily meant to be read from start to finish, but the list of contents should point you in the direction of what you want to know. I would also like to think that people in the manufacturing industries that support runners may take note of some of the issues I have raised, particularly with regard to clothing and equipment. I have focused on getting the right equipment, not necessarily the most expensive equipment, and on safety. The latter is particularly important for people venturing out on to trails and away from roads – although there is plenty that needs to be said about running safely on roads! I have signposted appropriate resources through books and websites.

So, what is stopping you? Get out into the fresh air. Get fit and enjoy your running safely.

Dr Gavin Spickett
DipEFL DipCBT MA BM BCh LLM DPhil
FRCPath FRCP FRCP(Edin)

1 | GETTING INTO RUNNING

There is plenty of evidence about the benefits of exercise and running. Despite this, there are plenty of naysayers who will try to discourage you. I shall discuss some of the problems that can arise from running but compared to the benefits, these are relatively small.

The main benefit of running will be general improvement in cardiovascular respiratory fitness. The blood flow to the heart and into the muscles will improve, which will also reduce the risks of arterial blockage. Impact exercise like running has a profoundly beneficial effect on preventing the development of osteoporosis or if osteopenia (thinning of bones before osteoporosis occurs) is present, then running will reverse it. Getting outdoors improves levels of vitamin D, and this contributes to protection of the bones, but also improves immunity and helps with depression. This will reduce the risk of premature fractures in old age.

Running has benefits for cognitive function and reduces the risk of Alzheimer's disease, particularly true for off-road running where a mental focus on balance and neuromuscular co-ordination is important. Running will help in a strategy to reduce weight and lower blood sugar, but only when combined with attention to diet. Runners overall live longer and have reduced risks of strokes, heart attacks and most types of cancer. There is no convincing scientific evidence that running is the primary cause of arthritis, although if the arthritis is present for other reasons it may make it worse. Running has demonstrable mental health benefits, especially for depression.

The message is clear: you can achieve significant and personally satisfying goals through running and you will reap long-term health benefits.

THE 'WHY'

Everyone has a reason for starting running. Whatever drives you to think about running will be personal to you. The most common reasons for wanting to take up running tend to be related to concerns about weight; new health issues such as type two diabetes; heart and lung problems; as a response to life stress or as part of a general re-evaluation of life goals. To run successfully, there needs to be considerable motivation maintained over a long period of time. It is useful to have clear goals – targeted weight loss, improvement of physical health, or perhaps most powerfully to raise money for charities, perhaps in memory of a lost one or for a personally meaningful cause. It can be helpful to set a target to aim for, but this needs to be a realistic target, for example completing a 5k parkrun or something more ambitious. You need to ensure that you have plenty of time to do the necessary training to get you to a level where you will be able to achieve your goal in an enjoyable fashion.

Age is no bar to taking up running (with appropriate medical cautions), and certainly continuing running past retirement age is both possible and excellent for health. You may not be as fast as the youngsters, but you may well be better over longer distances. Care with warm-up and cool-down regimes is more important as you age, to prevent injury.

What tends to work poorly are New Year resolutions with general goals such as to 'get fit'. In much the same way as gyms make most of their money in the first three months of the year, because of people making New Year's resolutions which they then don't keep, runners who start in the depths of winter without clear targets and goals are unlikely to stick at running in the long term. No one can hide the fact that for someone who has no history of running, getting out and starting running is going to be hard and requires meaningful motivation to keep going in the early stages, when it is most difficult.

There is a mass of scientific evidence which confirms the benefits of running. Other benefits are that as a hobby it is relatively cheap and easy to do and you can get outside and enjoy nature. It can be done virtually anywhere. It allows you to set challenges for yourself and gives you the satisfaction of achieving things that perhaps you never thought you could do (run a marathon?). You can start at any age.

This book is the accumulated wisdom, usually through making mistakes, of 30 years of running. My own start in running was much the same as many other people, so I know how hard it is trying to make the transition from an overweight sedentary adult to a fit and active runner.

My own journey began around the time of my 40th birthday, when I realised I had to take

BENEFITS OF RUNNING

- Living longer
- Reduced risks of heart disease, stroke, diabetes
- Reduced risk of developing Alzheimer's or dementia
- Reduced risk of some types of cancer
- Improved bone density (assuming dietary calcium and vitamin D intake are adequate)
- Boosts vitamin D levels in the summer
- Improved mental health (reduced stress, improved happiness)

serious action then if I wanted to avoid being significantly obese in ten years' time. I was predominantly sedentary, apart from a little walking. At that stage in my career, workload was manageable. I started running round my village – a fairly flat circuit of about one third of a mile. To begin with I could barely do more than one or two laps. I persevered and gradually the number of laps increased.

Our village is built on the side of the Tyne Valley. Once I was able to manage four circuits,

'The message is clear: you can achieve significant and personally satisfying goals through running, and you will reap long-term health benefits'

I started gradually trying to run up one of the main hills out of the village. This was a very slow process and the hill itself is nearly a mile. It took me three months of daily running trying to push up the hill a little bit further each day before I reached the top. For me, this was a massive achievement.

The next stage came when a work colleague suggested I should try the Great North Run, our iconic half marathon. In those days, there was nothing like ballots for places so getting in was quite straightforward. I joined the local running club to train, of which I've been a member ever since. I completed the Great North Run in a not very special time and have worked up to marathons and ultras. As age started catching up with me, I made the switch to trail running as it is easier on the joints. My story is not in any way remarkable. It never fails to move me when I read about the people who have gone from being clinically obese to being regular competitive runners, or those who have been able to turn getting fit into raising staggering sums of money for charity.

TIPS FOR STARTING RUNNING

- Identify a strong motivation
- Choose an appropriate time/place
- Get support from friends and family
- Be prepared to take your time
- Run/walk is a great way to start
- Get simple inexpensive clothing and shoes
- Stick at it!

WEIGHT LOSS AND RUNNING

A word of caution here. Many people start running as part of a weight-loss strategy. However, it is important to recognise that starting any form of consistent exercise programme will increase muscle size: muscle is heavier than fat and while in the early stages there will be

RUNNING AND WEIGHT LOSS

- Running by itself will not necessarily lead to weight loss
- Reduce calorie intake and choose healthy foods
- Avoid extreme diets when starting to run
- Avoid 'rewarding' runs with high-calorie snacks
- Focus on getting fit – weight loss will follow

loss of fat if food intake is appropriate, there will come a point when muscle bulk increases and the rate of weight loss will slow down. People get very disillusioned at this stage and will sometimes give up. What changes most is body shape. Bad fat (visceral fat within the abdomen) decreases and pot bellies recede. It is important to keep this in mind and not to give up.

There are any number of diets which claim to cause rapid weight loss and undoubtedly some of these do, often by reducing calorific intake to extremely low levels and by restricting fluid intake, clearly undesirable for running. If you are starting to run to help with dietary control for weight, it is important to ensure that your diet is properly balanced. If you have any concerns you should consult a trained state-registered dietician. It is important that the dietician fully understands your goals and your exercise plan. Weight loss of 1–2lb per week is likely to lead to a sustainable long-term change in weight (see 'Nutrition', Chapter 4).

Overall, the science is swinging towards focusing on getting fit rather than weight loss, as this tends to lead to greater long-term health benefits.

THE 'HOW'

If starting with no previous experience of running, turning motivation into action can be extremely hard. It is good to have support and encouragement from friends and family, as this will help through the difficult early stages. Make sure that people know what you're doing and why. If you are planning to get fit for participation in a charity fundraising event, get people involved early because this will give you additional motivation as you see the list of those who are prepared to donate money for your endeavours. Knowing that people support you will help you get out of the front door when the weather is foul.

If you have never run before and have any health issues or know that you are significantly overweight, then it is prudent to arrange a check with your GP before starting exercising. Get them to check your blood pressure. There are no absolute contraindications to exercise but there may be precautions required.

To begin with, only very basic equipment is required. Wear comfortable and loose-fitting clothes. For women, getting a supportive sports bra is advisable. There is no point in buying expensive trainers at the beginning, but they should be comfortable and supportive and it is essential they fit properly. Painful feet or blisters early on is likely to be highly demotivating. I cannot recommend strongly enough going to a proper running shop for advice about foot-wear. Use the trainers only for running, as the cushioning becomes degraded over time. The best shoes should be comfortable from the very outset. If they are not comfortable in the shop, they will never be comfortable.

Assuming that nothing untoward has been flagged up by your GP, then you can start making plans about how to get started. It is important to set a regular scheme on a daily basis so that exercise simply becomes part of your normal everyday routine. Do not allow anything else to interfere with the time set aside – this is 'me-time' and is sacrosanct. If you do not, you will fail to establish a regular pattern. To begin with, you need no more than ten to fifteen minutes. Choose a time of day which suits your lifestyle: are you a lark or an

DO NOT START RUNNING IF YOU HAVE

- High blood pressure
- Irregular heart beat
- Unexplained chest pains, especially on exertion
- Other significant medical problems

Wait until you have discussed your plans with your doctor.

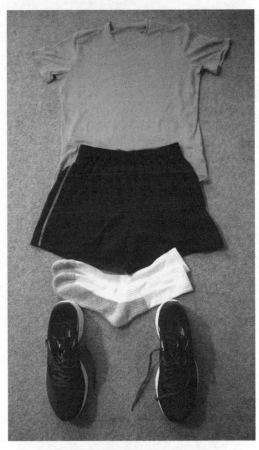

Basic running kit: T-shirt/shorts or tights/socks/shoes and fresh air.

owl? One of the best things about running is that it is entirely flexible: just put your shoes on, open the door and go!

Warm-up exercises: It is essential to do good warm-up exercises before running to get the heart rate up, blood circulating and the muscles warm. 1: Upper body twists; 2: Squats; 3: Arm swings; 4: Heel flicks. Other useful exercises include toe touches and running on the spot with knee lifts.

If you have never run before it makes sense to do some basic exercises before you start. This will help you avoid injury. Basic exercises can include squats, lunges, hip extensions (also known as bridges) and calf raises. None of these exercises require any special equipment (*see* 'Warm up and cool down', Chapter 5). However, good technique is essential. *Runner's World* website has videos of how to do each of these exercises.

Before each run, you should do a warm-up. The aim of this is to get the muscles moving and raise the heart rate to increase blood flow to the muscles. Each run should start slowly and then be at an even pace. You can slow down or walk on hills. The distance and time are initially not important. Try to get into a routine of exercising but don't beat yourself up if you miss days. At the end of each run, do a cool-down – this can just be a short period of brisk walking.

One of the biggest deterrents to exercise tends to be embarrassment about body shape and size. You need to be proud of the fact that you are getting out and exercising. If possible, persuade a friend to join you on your running endeavours. If you do feel body conscious, use loose-fitting clothing to begin with. Your first efforts will be very short, and do not be afraid to mix walking and running. Even for famous and experienced runners doing ultramarathons, walking plays an essential part. Walking

---

DYNAMIC WARM-UP EXERCISES

- Arm swings
- Upper body twists
- Hip bends to touch toes
- Squats
- Lunges
- Calf raises
- Jogging on the spot with heel flicks or high knees

---

up steep hills is far more energy efficient than trying to run up them. Walking in this setting needs to be active walking, brisk enough to impact on your pulse rate.

You will need to be patient, as the increase in fitness will develop slowly and only with regular exercise. Do not expect a miraculous reduction in your weight: this will follow in due course. Weight loss also requires attention to diet. Exercise without a change in the diet is not likely to be successful in reducing weight.

If you are worried about motivation, another way of getting into running is through an outdoor fitness class. Again, new starters tend to be anxious that they will be joining a class where there are lots of superfit people. All the classes that I have attended have had good instructors who will set tasks for beginners, intermediates and advanced participants so that everybody gets to join in. In my experience, long-standing members of the classes have always been extremely welcoming. Everybody remembers how it was when they first started, and everybody will applaud that you have made the effort to join the class.

While attention to diet is important, do not try to start running at the same time as beginning an extreme diet. Just try to cut down a little. Smaller helpings will gradually train your stomach to feel full with less (*see* 'Nutrition', Chapter 4). Looking at the composition of the diet is also important. Everyone will require a balance of protein, fat and carbohydrate.

'Do not allow anything else to interfere with the time set aside for exercise – this is "me-time" and is sacrosanct'

If your motivation to start running is not weight or health, the same basic principles apply in terms of starting off with simple equipment and using a walk/run technique. At the beginning you will not need to increase your food and calorie intake. Rather disappointingly there are enough calories in two digestive biscuits to fuel you for a considerable run.

Some people find listening to music helpful to maintain motivation during runs. Wearing headphones however reduces your situational awareness of hazards. Headphones (except bone conduction headphones) are banned in all England Athletics road races. Why not enjoy nature and focus on being in the moment?

Motivation can also be improved by choosing different places to run. Forestry England have waymarked run routes of varying distances in some of their forests and the National Trust do the same. Both organise their own runs, which is a good way to find out about new routes safely. Parkruns are also a way of finding new routes: all abilities take part.

When you start exercising, you can expect that your muscles will be sore. This will usually be the next day or the one after. Unless the pain or discomfort is severe, you can continue to exercise at the same level. Gradually this discomfort will improve and this is the point at which you can start increasing the distance. If there is severe pain, you should stop and rest

HOW TO MAINTAIN MOTIVATION

- Set aside 'me' time
- Get into a regular routine
- Find a friend to come with you or go to a parkrun
- Listen to music (but retain situational awareness)
- Be prepared to go out whatever the weather
- Warm up before running to avoid injury
- Accept the aches as normal
- Timetable rest days

> '*Do not think you can do a couple of runs and then turn up for the Great North Run half-marathon*'

until it has subsided. It is important to build up the level of exercise quite slowly to allow your muscles, heart and lungs to adjust. Trying to do too much too quickly will inevitably lead to problems and is likely to reduce motivation. You may well have set a particular goal, such as a particular event, so make sure you have left yourself a reasonable amount of time to reach the required level. Running magazines and online sites have a range of 'Couch to...' programmes for most event distances. The longer the event, the longer you need to allow for the training. Do not think you can do a couple of runs and then turn up for the Great North Run half-marathon.

Do not get hung up on running particular distances on a particular day, or running so many miles per week. We all have good days and bad days and if it is a bad day, cutting the run short is best. However, it is important to try to establish a regular routine and stick to it, even if it is only a short run. This helps maintain motivation. Running everyday isn't essential. Do not feel guilty or beat yourself up if your session is short or you miss a session. Even if you can't do a run, try to get outside and do a walk instead. Allow yourself a (small) treat for recovery. Running does get easier the more you do, but then you can up the challenges.

If you are starting out and are an older person, then you need to make allowances for this and have longer warm-ups and cooldowns. Doing strength and conditioning is more important. Getting older does not automatically mean getting slower: with the correct training and, if necessary, gait analysis, it is perfectly possible to increase your speed and endurance. As we live longer there are more and more examples of very elderly athletes (even into their 90s or centenarians) running remarkably fast or running long distances (such as marathons) or doing the ultimate endurance event: Ironman Triathlons.

This book is not about providing specific day-by-day guidance on training programmes: running magazines such as *Runners' World*, the internet and various books address this far better than I can. The published programmes have usually been produced by experienced run fitness trainers. I shall however cover a range of aspects to consider about training and fitness programmes in later chapters.

HOW TO PROGRESS

Progression in running is going to be dependent upon personal goals and motivation. There is no doubt that the fundamental issue is not going to be about the legs but about the head. Many people get fit for a specific event only, with no long-term expectation of continuing to run. However, some people are captivated by running once they start and carry on. This can be driven by what is commonly known as the 'runner's high'. The body releases a range of compounds during and immediately after running which produce a euphoriant effect. These include endorphins, which are the body's equivalent of morphine (heroin), and endocannabinoids, which are the equivalent of cannabis. These substances assist in coping with the stresses and pain from running. This means that running can be addictive and people who have been running regularly and suddenly stop may suffer what might be described as withdrawal symptoms, which can make it quite hard dealing with illness and injury and means that people will often run when they should be resting.

'Be kind to yourself and remember to see the positives of what you have achieved and do not dwell on the negatives'

The next stage in your running career is going to be to determine how running will fit in to your life. Many people are quite happy to just go out with friends simply for the benefits of running and for social reasons. Not everyone wants to go to races and not everybody wants to explore their body's limits. If you're happy being a social runner, there is plenty in this book in terms of advice about equipment and nutrition and you should go out and enjoy your running. Please however make sure that you take steps to avoid injury and ensure that your social running is safe.

Progression always requires motivation: remember why you started running. Have a mantra to recite to help your motivation. Use visualisation techniques, imagining yourself running gracefully without effort. If you set a routine, running becomes easier. Try to avoid negative thoughts. Starting a run is always hard, so don't let that negative thought block you from getting out and running. No one ever said that running was easy, but achieving things that are not easy is important for boosting self-confidence, as is keeping track of your achievements.

Be kind to yourself and remember to see the positives of what you have achieved and do not dwell on the negatives. Try always to have a set of achievable goals, short term, medium term and long term. Always re-evaluate your progress against the goals and don't be afraid to modify them: that is not failure, that is sensible running. Do not get locked into goals such as 'I must run 20 miles a week' – this can be too prescriptive. Be flexible. A week with shorter, faster runs is just as good or better than churning out slow runs just to meet an arbitrary mileage target ('junk' miles). As you progress it is important to think about how you train; this needs to be appropriate to your goals and you should avoid getting obsessed. Three to five sessions (running or other fitness training) per week is more than adequate. Trying to run just once a week with no other activity will be difficult and is not likely to lead to much improvement.

For those bitten by the running bug, the next stage will be to look at what else is available. If you plan on making running a more serious hobby, then paying attention to equipment, nutrition and hydration and training as well as injury prevention is critical to gain the maximum enjoyment. Many people starting out will be fearful that they will be embarrassed going to races because that's where all the superfit people will be. It is not true; races cater for all abilities. So what if you come last – some people will not even have finished and many never even started – be proud that you finished.

Remember that in the races you are really competing against yourself, and entering for the enjoyment of going to new places and

HOW TO PROGRESS

- Set realistic, achievable targets
- Get into a routine
- Remind yourself why you started running
- Set time aside
- Do not get fixated on running a particular distance each week
- Do other fitness activities as well
- Enjoy your running

'Maintain motivation and get support through virtual or local running clubs, social media and friends but avoid compare and despair'

meeting new people who share your interest. If you have discovered a natural talent for running, there is plenty of scope for testing yourself out against the best in your region or possibly nationally. Whichever category you fall into, you still need to apply the basic rules of equipment, nutrition and hydration, and training and injury prevention.

Joining a local running club is a good place to start. As well as being a way to meet other people, having the same interest is also the scope for structured training and social events. Again, new runners will be anxious that running clubs are the preserve of the superfit but this is not true: all running clubs cater for all grades of runner and all will welcome new members. There are also a number of online virtual running clubs such as Run Things and Lonely Goat, and clubs for specific groups (*see* Resources).

If you run regularly with a running club or group it can get competitive and this can increase the risk of injuries, so it is important not to be dragged into doing runs that you know are beyond you. The flip side is that being in a group may make you push your boundaries. Don't be afraid to give training a miss to have a recovery period. Group runs will lock you into a routine, which can be good and bad: it will make you more likely to get out and run it but equally it might be difficult to fit in with other things in your life. Being part of a group gives a source of running advice from the 'been there, done that and got the T-shirt' brigade. However, such advice may be tainted with incorrect running myths, so it is worth sense-checking what you hear. Always think critically about anything you hear or read. Does it make sense for you?

Being a member of a running club will mean that you have registered with England Athletics. This will give you a discount on the entry fee to affiliated races and discounts for various equipment and clothing providers. If you plan on doing a few affiliated road races each year, the discount for EA members will more than cover the costs of the annual registration fee. Not all races are affiliated to EA and most trail races will not offer a discount.

If you don't fancy joining a club and just like to go out with your friends, you might consider doing virtual challenges. You can usually do these at a time and place of your choosing. Some will require you to submit evidence (such as from a GPS watch or Strava). You can choose between one-off events and events over months or much longer distances. Some will accept lots of different types of exercise (walking, running, biking, swimming) and will accept teams. Again, these will help maintain motivation.

Running magazines provide another useful source of information and inspiration. *Runner's World* is the best known, but there are *Men's Running*, *Women's Running* and *Trail Running* (now subsumed into *Trail* magazine sadly). *Runner's World* is available in print and digitally, but the others are digital only. *Ultra* is a print magazine covering running beyond marathons.

MEDICAL CAUTIONS

If you have any underlying medical conditions and wish to start running, it is advisable to have a medical check and discussion with your GP. This is particularly important if you have any history of heart disease, high blood pressure, diabetes, kidney disease or if you are seriously overweight. In almost all circumstances, cautious exercise will be beneficial to the underlying medical conditions but the approach to getting fit may need to be much slower. If you are on regular medication, it is also worth discussing with your GP whether this will have any impact on your fitness regime. For example, beta-blockers will slow the heart rate down and make it much harder to achieve the maximum predicted heart rate on exercise. Diuretic tablets (water tablets) will increase your risk of dehydration in hot weather. If you have arthritis and are taking anti-inflammatory tablets (ibuprofen and similar), these will interfere with kidney function, particularly if you get dehydrated, and may be more likely to cause bleeding from the bowel if you exercise hard.

Asthma can cause some problems and you may need to have your inhalers modified. A lot of asthmatics find when they start running their chest will get quite tight, but then as they continue this improves. Some have asthma that is specifically triggered by exercise, but this can be helped by using the reliever inhaler before running.

If you have already started running and developed any new symptoms, particularly new chest pain or pain radiating from the chest to the neck, the arms or the back while exercising, then you should **stop exercising immediately** until you have consulted your GP.

Every so often there are reports in the media of apparently fit people with no medical history collapsing and sometimes dying while exercising. These rare cases are usually due to unsuspected and genetically determined diseases of the heart muscle. Anyone contemplating an exercise programme who has a family history, however remote, of sudden unexplained death at an early age is strongly advised to consult their GP **before** undertaking strenuous activity.

DISABILITY

Disability is no bar to running or fitness training and discrimination is not permitted where reasonable adjustments can be made to enable participation. The successes of Paralympians show just how much can be achieved. Depending on the disability, it will be advisable to discuss plans for running with your medical advisers. It also makes sense to get assistance from a trainer with knowledge of disability. Exercise is just as important for disabled people as for non-disabled, if not more so. It may be advisable to work on strength training and balance exercises, before introducing running, depending on the type of disability. Disability includes those with intellectual impairment or some mental health issues as well as physical disabilities.

For those with lower-limb amputations, the key will be getting advice from the prosthetist about the best limb prosthesis for running and making sure that it fits properly and does not rub. The prosthesis may need regular adjustment as weight and muscle bulk change. Participation in running events in race wheelchairs is also possible, but it is important to check with organisers early on.

For those who are blind or partially sighted, guide runners may be used who are linked to the blind runner and can provide a commentary on hazards. Guides can be found through England Athletics (*see* Resources). For those with hearing impairment, it is important to have a pencil and paper to write questions and ensure that any run leader has agreed visual signals in advance. Runners with a learning disability often benefit from having a running buddy who knows them well to provide support.

England Athletics and Disability Sport England have plenty of advice, including for coaches and running clubs. Scope, the charity for the disabled, can provide advice on facilities available locally (*see* Resources).

SOCIAL MEDIA

Many events and running groups have their own social media sites which give you a flavour of how they work. Such groups can be a useful source of advice about how to approach an event, what shoes to wear, where to stay and so on – the sort of questions that you can't really ask the organiser. Advice is freely offered by those who have done the event before. For some events, key race information may be posted on their Facebook page, and after the race, photos may be uploaded. Virtual running clubs will function mainly through social media and can provide vital encouragement and support.

CHARITIES

Many people start running to raise money for personally meaningful charities. Large charities will often have an allocation of places for major events such as the London Marathon, which you can apply for if not successful in open ballots. The downside is that you will be committing to raise a minimum sum for the charity. Smaller charities will be less likely to have places and will have less support. If you are doing a race for a charity, let the organisers know: they may give you a shout-out at the start or finish. Put it on your social media site and, if possible, have a Just Giving or equivalent page, so that it is easy for people to support you. Having a target to raise and knowing that others are supporting your efforts are powerful motivators.

2 | WHERE NEXT?

Once you have started running, you will probably find that it is quite addictive, due to the release of endorphins. Try to avoid allowing running to consume your life. However, some people become disillusioned. Often it is due to setting unrealistic and unattainable goals or simply that life gets in the way. The key to progressing is to maintain motivation: running clubs have a role here. It is best to join a running group which fits your aims.

Try to be flexible in your training and do not obsess about miles, times, number of training sessions and so on. Sports watches which give you training tips can help but can lead to a feeling that you are a slave to the watch. Feel free to run when you want, as fast or as slow as you want. Doing a run without looking at your watch is good, so you can learn to recognise pace without relying on it. Even a short run is better than no run. Winter always produces a challenge. Provided that you equip yourself with the most appropriate winter and night-running clothing (*see* Chapter 3), winter running can be quite invigorating and represents a challenge in its own right. Remember, the primary reasons for running are to enjoy it, get fitter and challenge yourself.

If you have been running for a while and the motivation is diminishing, sometimes having a complete break and doing something completely different is helpful. This happens to everyone: do not get miserable – just do something else and come back to running when you feel like it. The important thing is to try not to just stay in your comfort zone if you want to progress. Set new goals: to run in new places, to run faster, to run more frequently.

Setting realistic and achievable goals is very important. These should include new challenges. Think about different types of running and different events. Whatever you plan to do, it should be your plan, not someone else's. By all means use a published plan, but adapt it to suit your needs: 'own' the plan. Don't forget

'Set new goals: to run in new places, to run faster, to run more frequently'

that doing other sorts of fitness activities breaks up the running and contributes to getting fit, for example cycling, fitness classes, swimming or hiking. Divide goals into short, medium and long term: write them down and remind yourself of them regularly.

PARKRUNS

Parkruns were originally started to help people get out and get fit as well as to raise money for charities. The movement started in the UK but has now become a worldwide phenomenon, with parkruns now available across the globe. Entry is free and registration only has to be done once, after which you can turn up to any event. The runs are 5km for adults and 2km for children. These runs are excellent and a sociable way of getting into running with the whole family. Some people specifically focus on doing as many different parkruns as they can and building parkruns into holiday schedules.

The success of the parkrun movement is a testimony to how much it fulfils a need. The fact that entry is free means that no one is excluded on financial grounds. It is a great way to get into running events and for many people it is all that they ever need or want. Because there are parkruns everywhere, you can drop into local ones wherever you are.

ROAD RUNNING

Most of us will do a large proportion of our running on roads. When I started my running career, alternatives to road running were limited and were the preserve of fairly small groups of specialist runners, for example fell runners or some of the early ultra-trail runners. This has now changed and there is a much wider variety of runs on different surfaces and of every conceivable distance.

Road running has the advantage that the surfaces are usually reasonably safe and flat, although minor roads may have potholes and other hazards. Pavements are equally badly maintained. One complication of running on roads is that they often have a camber, the road is higher in the middle and if this is significant, it can gave rise to biomechanical problems because you will be running continuously across a fixed slope. Running continuously on hard surfaces will be harder on the feet and it is essential to make sure that your footwear is appropriate both for the feet and for the surface. Adequate cushioning, especially if you are a heavier runner, is sensible. Road surfaces will be abrasive and will wear down the outsole at the point of impact. Some shoe manufacturers will specifically reinforce the impact area on the heel with more resistant rubber.

There are large numbers of road races on offer. You can look up areas of interest on the internet, or magazines such as *Runner's World* and *Trail Running* will have calendars and advertisements for major events.

There will be entry fees. The costs have risen steeply over the last few years, as organisers' costs have risen. The most popular events sell out rapidly, or require you to enter a ballot. This can mean that you are paying upfront for an event that may not happen for months, so check the organiser's policy for refunds. Some of the most expensive races offer the option to insure the cost if you are unable to participate. Many events offer early-bird price reductions, which can be significant, or reduced entry prices for entering a series of events.

TRAIL RUNNING

The term 'trail running' applies to any off-road running. This may be on prepared trails or rougher footpaths and bridleways. We are very lucky in this country to have a large network of paths and tracks, clearly shown on Ordnance Survey maps. The running surface is likely to be uneven, with hazards such as rocks and tree roots. Trail running is excellent for improving balance and co-ordination and requires a degree of concentration. Expect that trails will be wet and muddy, especially in winter. Off-road shoes are a must. These will have extra rubber protection for the toes and heel, should have an integrated tongue, which reduces the amount of dirt entering the shoe, and will have a tougher outsole with longer lugs for grip (*see* 'Shoes', Chapter 3). Because the ground is (usually) softer, the impact effect on joints and muscles is less.

A lot of forests, especially those managed by Forestry England and the National Trust, have excellent trails, which are waymarked, and they also support regular trail races. Forest running can be quite soft but can still be uneven with rocks and hidden tree roots.

In many parts of the country, trail running will incorporate hill ascents and descents

'Trail running is excellent for improving balance and co-ordination and requires a degree of concentration'

and in areas like the Lake District and North York Moors, trail runs blur into mountain running. Specific training is required to cope with this type of terrain. Many trails will have steep sections both up and down, as well as muddy/boggy sections. Terrain underfoot will vary from soft to hard irregular rock.

Trail running is more relaxing in the sense that there is no traffic, and you get to see the countryside. The major hazards are the terrain and other trail users: not all cyclists are considerate to runners.

Trail running can take you to spectacular countryside, such as the Lake District.

There are plenty of trail races across a whole range of distances and like road races, these are now organised by specific event groups. Most will be well signposted and marshalled, with aid stations and on-call first aid response teams. Some events will have specific mandatory kit requirements. Even if you are not entering a race but just running by yourself or with friends, it is worth considering taking extra kit with you in case of emergencies (*see* 'Mandatory equipment', Chapter 3). Entry for trail races is much the same as for road races.

OBSTACLE AND THEMED EVENTS

Over the last ten to fifteen years there has been an upsurge of interest in more challenging events loosely classified as obstacle races across varying terrain. These will include obstacles to climb over or under and will generally involve other unpleasantness such as freezing cold water, deep mud, and even fire. You can assume that by the time you reach the finish you will not only be tired but filthy from head to toe.

There are a wide variety of events to choose from and there are world championship series for the super achievers. However, there is plenty of scope for the weekend warriors to get out and have fun. The best known are the Tough Mudder series and the Spartan series (*see* Resources), both of which have events worldwide. There are other more local events as well.

Unlike straightforward trail runs, these obstacle events will require significant upper body strength for climbing over the obstacles or carrying heavy weights. It is essential to make sure that you have had appropriate strength training beforehand. Getting over some of the obstacles may require teamwork. While there tends to be good camaraderie at the events so that strangers will help other strangers, it is worthwhile entering with a friend or as a team and going round together.

Obstacle races can leave you muddy from head to toe! Reproduced with permission of Anne Harper.

CROSS-COUNTRY AND HARRIER LEAGUES

Cross-country running is an individual or team sport, usually undertaken in the winter, over short-to-medium courses of 2.5–7.5 miles.

Terrain is usually fields, tracks and woodland, with minor obstacles. Runners can compete as individuals but most compete as part of their running club teams for points, with a performance league (harrier league). Footwear tends to comprise cross-country spikes, metal spikes of varying lengths, determined by the terrain. The sport has a long history going back to the mid-nineteenth century. There are international championships, and it forms part of the modern pentathlon in the Olympic games. The races usually take place whatever the weather.

FELL AND MOUNTAIN RUNNING

Fell running has a long history, mostly localised to the UK's major upland areas such as the Lake District and Peak District. Often, the events were linked to the agricultural shows, an essential part of the rural community where farmers and farm workers would come together and which would sometimes culminate in a race up the Fells. Initially routes tended to be vertical climbs followed by equally vertical descents, all done at high speed, usually wearing nothing more than singlet, shorts and basic fell-running shoes. This would not be over well-manicured tracks. The distances on the whole are quite short but the ascents are significant. Races are graded on their ascent and distance by the Fell Runners Association.

The longer fell races have morphed into mountain running and skyrunning as a separate discipline, combining ultra-distance events over mountainous terrain. Mountain running is essentially trail running on defined tracks and avoiding dangerous sections. Sections may be on roads. Mountain marathons are similar but are usually two-day events, with competitors required to carry all their overnight equipment and compete as a team of two, visiting defined way points. Navigation and survival skills are essential, a cross between mountain running and orienteering. Skyrunning was developed by alpine climbers in the early 1990s and now encompasses races at high level across the globe. It is defined as running above 2,000m, where the minimum average incline is 6 per cent over the total distance and at least 5 per cent has an incline of 30 per cent.

RUNNING WITH YOUR DOG — CANICROSS

Some trail races allow you to take your dog, but check with the organisers. There are organised races (canicross) where you and your dog are harnessed together and usually compete over a trail course (*see* Resources). Before entering these races, you need to ensure that your dog is properly socialised. Your dog will need specific training to voice and hand commands.

Just as you have to train to compete, the dog will need training in exactly the same way, building up its general fitness to begin with, starting with increasing walk distances on variable terrain to harden up the pads. The dog should have a canicross harness which has the attachment clip towards the back of the body, allowing its shoulders to move freely. You will also need to have an appropriate waist harness to which the dog can be attached. Kisi produce some excellent gear (*see* Resources).

Interestingly studies of dogs taking part in canicross events with their owners have shown that where the owners may be working at maximum oxygen consumption (VO_2 max), a trained dog may well only be working at a third of maximal capacity. This is rather disillusioning for the human.

When running with dogs it is essential to pay great attention to the weather and in particular the heat and humidity. Make sure that you do training runs when it is colder first thing in the morning or in the evening or try out routes, for example through woods where there is adequate shade. Just as you would take water for yourself, do not forget your canine friend. Do not rely on finding clean streams and puddles. Dogs do not sweat except through their paws and can only cool themselves through panting. Do not run or even walk your dog on tarmac in hot sun as the tarmac can burn the pads. Equally in winter, make sure that your dog does not get too cold. Check your dog's paws at the end of each run for signs of injury. Ruff Wear provide excellent equipment for dogs including jackets and protective boots (*see* Resources).

Most canicross races will be in the autumn, winter and early spring.

ULTRARUNNING

Ultrarunning is anything over a marathon (>26.2 miles). The hardcore elite endurance runners are now pushing the boundaries of what we previously believed was possible. From events of 55k (approx. 34 miles), events go up to multiple-day endurance events of hundreds or even thousands of miles. These are seriously hard events, and need meticulous preparation plus proper support. The shorter ultras which can be completed in a day are the next step up from marathons. These will mostly be off-road although there are some road ultras (London to Brighton Race). Endurance Life, Lakeland Trails, Hardmoors and Threshold Trails all offer excellent, well organised and supported events (*see* Resources), and there are many more. Some of the events are very popular and sell out quickly.

> ## 'Anyone can run ultras, including older people'

Anyone can run ultras, including older people. Because the pace is much slower, older people can often do quite well, with appropriate preparation, and are often keen to set themselves new challenges. Angela White, aka the Running Granny (*see* Resources), is an example of someone coming to ultrarunning later in life. The legendary fell runner Joss Naylor continued to run prodigious distances into his 80s.

If you are planning to do an ultra, you need to know that you can do a marathon (although not everyone seems to bother with this step). Equally if you can cope with a marathon, then there is no reason why you can't cope with an ultra. Go up in steps and choose an ultra with sensible cut-offs that you know you can achieve. Look for the level of support and professionalism from the organisers. Think about the time of year. If you plan to do an event where extremes of temperature are likely (Antarctic, Sahara), then getting professional advice on training for the environment is mandatory. Give yourself plenty of time to train and build up the training slowly to avoid injury.

The main factor in success at ultrarunning is the mental stamina to cope with exceptionally long runs when you are alone, in pain, cold, wet (potentially), miserable, hungry, thirsty and sleep deprived. Some people say of ultrarunners that they do it to test the boundaries of what is personally possible, to push further and further until they fail. Training for ultras therefore is not just about training to put one foot in front of the other for unreasonable distances, but training your mind to cope with the pain and misery.

WINTER RUNNING

Running in winter requires some additional care and attention but can be great fun. Getting out running in the winter helps beat the winter blues. Road, trail and mountain races are scheduled throughout the year. For road running, icy conditions can be dangerous, particularly where black ice may occur. If conditions are very icy, road races may be cancelled. Off-road running is easier and running in snow can be fun, but beware of icy and slippery rocks.

In winter, heavy rain may be an issue. Make sure that you have good-quality waterproofs.

Being out in the rain in the winter can contribute to becoming very cold very quickly: make sure you have adequate layers including some extra ones in a dry bag, and that essential gear (such as phone and keys) is in waterproof bags.

There are specific winter races, arranged to take place when the weather is likely to be

Out trail running in the snow. Beware of icy patches and make sure that your shoes have adequate treads to give grip.

bad. These are very likely to be off-road and to have very specific mandatory equipment requirements (*see* 'Mandatory equipment', Chapter 3).

VIRTUAL RUNNING CHALLENGES

The Covid pandemic decimated mass participation running events. Some events restarted with staggered start times, with strict rules for arrivals and departure which rather damaged the social side of participation. There has been a huge increase in virtual events, uploading evidence to the website. These include single-day events, but there are many multi-day challenges where distances must be completed over a fixed time. You can usually choose your distance and/or time frame. Some events offer options for hiking, swimming and running or allow combinations. Some virtual events allow you to watch your progress round a given geographic circuit, in a way that means you can compete against friends and family.

If this is something that is of interest. have a look at:

- Run Things: This organisation has a strong focus on raising money for charity and mental health, and has a number of events through the year, designed to appeal to everyone. These can be team events or solo efforts. You can join the club for a one-off payment and they will handle England Athletics (EA) registration on an annual basis.
- Race at Your Pace: These are month-long challenges where you choose from a pre-set target distance or personalise your own. This can be walking, running, swimming or cycling.
- Conqueror Challenges: Here you get the opportunity to complete named challenges around the world. For some you can see where you are using Google Streetview, and the organisers send you digital postcards with interesting information and pictures of places you pass through. They plant a tree for every 20 per cent of the challenge you complete.
- ACE Races: They have a range of races from 10k to 400k.
- Ultra Challenges: These are a set of challenges around the UK which can be done as physical or virtual challenges.
- Lakeland Trails: As well as an amazing series of trail races over a range of distances, they offer virtual events in the winter, with mapping of your progress round courses in the Lake District.
- Run Nation: Focusing mainly on road races, they have a virtual race offering too. They have a focus on the North of England (where they are based). They also have their own Run Club with EA affiliation.
- *Trail Running* magazine has an annual year-long Run 1,000 miles virtual challenge. There is a very active and supportive Facebook group.

Many other race organisers offer a combination of virtual and physical events, so there is plenty of choice. Having targets to reach is helpful for maintaining motivation and gives you something tangible for the training miles that you put in. Most of the sites have apps for mobile phones and/or will link to Strava for direct uploading of activities. Some events require evidence for completion, but others rely on your honesty, on the basis that the only person you are cheating is yourself. Most will have Facebook pages where you can link up with other people doing the same events.

3 | EQUIPMENT

A runner's main expense in equipment terms will be shoes and possibly a decent breathable waterproof jacket. Shoes may improve performance, but this will come at a price. Until you know you are hooked on running, it is best to stick to simple functional clothing – you can 'upgrade' later if you feel the need. Readers are strongly advised to research equipment thoroughly. Specialist running shops and fellow runners are good sources of advice.

If you are a member of a running club, there may well be discounts at running stores and the discounts may well cover the running club subscription with some to spare over a year. Whatever you wear, it needs to be comfortable and not too tight to start with. Flatlock seams are essential on tops and bottoms, so that they don't rub. Pre-used clothing can be obtained from ReRun, which collects unwanted running clothing for resale (*see* Resources).

SHOES

The choice is colossal and manufacturers often produce new versions every six months. Choosing the right shoe is critical to comfort, performance and possibly to reducing injury.

> *'Choosing the right shoe is critical to comfort, performance and possibly to reducing injury'*

The only way of being certain is to go to a specialist running shop and try lots of different shoes. Choose a running shop with room to run in the shoes or with a treadmill. Here are some golden rules.

BASIC EQUIPMENT TO START RUNNING

- T-shirt
- Shorts/leggings
- Proper sports bra
- Comfortable padded socks
- Basic pair of running shoes (correct size)

Of these, the shoes are the most important

Rule 1 – Know what you are going to use the shoe for

This might seem self-evident, but shoes for road, trails, fell-running, running on rocks, on mud and so on are all different.

If you use road shoes on trails, you will have no grip and risk falling. If you use rock-trail shoes with a protective rock-plate on roads for any length of time your feet will get very sore and you risk injury. Some shoes are made specifically as 'race shoes', usually stripped down with reduced cushioning. Do not use these for training as you will rapidly destroy the shoes and.may cause injury. If you want lightweight race shoes, keep them for races.

Magazines such as *Runner's World* and *Trail Running* do regular gear tests and reviews, and there are online review sites. However, as feet are individual, the reviews may not reflect how you may get on. Make sure you choose the right shoes for the terrain.

RIGHT SHOES FOR THE JOB

- Road shoes: usually lighter with flat soles and little protection around the toes. Racing shoes will have thinner soles and are stripped back. May have carbon fibre plates which will make them more rigid
- Trail shoes: heavier, more rigid, thicker outsole with lugs, toe protection
- Rocky trails and mountains: as for trail shoes but with more robust outsole and midsole rockplate (either full length or just under the forefoot); much more rigid
- Muddy trails: as for trail shoes but often narrower fit with long lugs

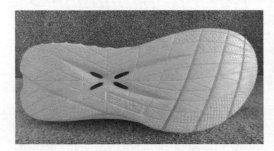

Road shoes will have relatively smooth soles with shallow or no tread. These will have no grip if used on trails and can slip if used on icy roads.

Trail shoes will have a more resilient outsole, often Vibram or equivalent with deeper lugs for grip. These will be uncomfortable when running for long periods on roads.

Shoes for muddy terrain will have much longer lugs and often have a very narrow fit, to reduce the risk of the shoes being pulled off in the mud. They are very uncomfortable for running on anything other than soft terrain.

Rule 2 – Go to a proper specialist running store

Unless you have bought and used exactly the same make and model before, or know that you can send them back if not suitable, don't order online.

Some stores will have treadmills and can do gait analysis, and this may help narrow the selection. Some outdoor stores which sell trail shoes will have a mock rock slope to test shoes: this is helpful to check how stable the shoes are on rough terrain up and down. If there isn't one, test the shoes by walking backwards. Do not be embarrassed to try on lots of different shoes: the assistants should be knowledgeable and will be pleased to get out half a dozen or more shoes for you to try on. If they just want to push one shoe on you, walk away and go somewhere else.

Rule 3 – Get the size right

Far too many people buy running shoes that are too small in length and too narrow. Running shoes will be ½–1 size larger than your everyday shoes. Be aware that manufacturers' interpretation of sizes is highly variable. You should have at least a full thumb's width between the end of the big toe and the end of the shoe. Check both feet. Check the width at the base of the toes: some manufacturers have wide versions of their shoes. There should be no feeling of pressure on the sides of the foot. The heel should be gripped comfortably, and should not move around. The sides of the heel

Go to a well-stocked running shop to choose shoes. It should have shoes from several different manufacturers and a runway to test the shoes out. With permission from Chivers Sports, Carlisle.

cuff and heel tab should not dig in or rub. Take time in the shop to get the lacing close to what you would normally want and make sure that the tongue is padded enough to be comfortable: some lightweight racing shoes skimp on the tongue, which means the laces can dig in as the foot swells during a run. Make sure that, if you have high arches, there is enough height in the shoe for your foot to sit comfortably.

Run up and down. If the shoe is too short, your toes will bang against the front, especially running downhill and this will contribute to black toenails, or even loss of toenails. If the shoe is too narrow, then you run the risk of blisters. The shoes need to be comfortably fitting all round, but the whole foot needs to be supported, especially around the ankle. The forefoot should not slide around in the shoe. It is particularly important to get the fit right for trail shoes, as uneven tracks will create more twisting strain. Shoes for use on muddy terrain are usually a much narrower fit, with grip around the heels to reduce the risk of the shoes being sucked off in deep mud.

When trying shoes, be aware that your feet swell as the day goes on. If you try shoes on in the morning, wear thicker socks. Think about what socks you will be using to run in.

If you are planning to do ultra events, your feet will swell significantly during the course of the run. Some events allow you to have drop bags at checkpoints. It may be worth getting two pairs of the same shoes, but with half a size difference, so you can swap to a larger shoe halfway through. Alternatively, just have the large shoe and wear thick socks for the first half, then change to thin socks.

Rule 4 – If it isn't comfortable immediately in the shop, then it will never be comfortable

All the evidence suggests that a shoe that is immediately comfortable in the shop will be right for you. Research has shown that trying to pick shoes according to foot type makes no

difference and that people do best just choosing the shoe that feels most comfortable. People naturally choose shoes that seem to be the best fit for their running style, and which give the most economic gait. So, while gait analysis is helpful, on-foot comfort rules supreme. The best shoes should feel like a slipper – I use the most comfortable ones as slippers/recovery shoes when they are past their running best.

Do not think that shoes need to be 'run-in' to be comfortable. This is a fallacy. The best shoes are the ones that you can put on and go straight out for a long run and come back with no blisters or black toes. If you can't do this, then you need to be looking for a different shoe. The only exception is shoes with

'Do not think that shoes need to be "run-in" to be comfortable. This is a fallacy'

carbon fibre plates, which can be very stiff to begin with but relax a little with use.

Do however do training runs in new shoes before you use them in a race, to make sure there are no niggles.

Rule 5 – The cushioning in the midsole of running shoes wears out

The midsole of the shoe is the section which provides the cushioning and the return of energy when your foot hits the ground. Most running shoes will last somewhere between 250–400 miles before the cushioning degrades. Some makers now claim mileages of up to 1,200 miles. There is no magic figure for the mileage at which you should replace shoes. Continuing to use running shoes when the midsole has lost its elasticity is an invitation to injury. The midsoles will recover better if they are allowed time to regain their original shape after a run.

If you can afford it, getting two pairs of running shoes and alternating them actually works out as a cost saving in the long term as each pair will last longer in terms of mileage than they would if used as the only shoe. While initially the foam in the midsole will bounce back to its original shape quite quickly, as the shoes wear the foam rebounds more slowly and not to 100 per cent of its starting shape. There is also a suggestion that alternating shoes reduces the risk of injury. Ideally use two similar pairs of shoes, but from different manufacturers. The slight differences may reduce repetitive strain, by altering very slightly your foot dynamics while running.

Do not use road shoes for rough trail runs, as this will degrade the structure more quickly. Equally do not use trail shoes on roads for extended periods, as they will be uncomfortable (they tend to be stiffer than road shoes, to cope with undulating and rocky terrain). Do not use your running shoes for general walking around: this will wear them out faster.

Rule 6 – Get the correct heel-to-toe drop and stack height

Another very confusing area is the heel-to-toe drop, the difference in height between the thickness of the heel and the thickness of the forefoot. The usual range for this figure will be 0 to 12mm. The zero drop shoes effectively equate to running barefoot. A 12mm drop is quite high; most runners will find the extremes of the range are uncomfortable and may increase the risk of hip and knee pain. Most runners will be most comfortable in the range of 4–8mm. If you know that you have very tight calf muscles or short Achilles tendons, do not go for very low-drop shoes as these will be extremely uncomfortable and increase your risk of injury. If you wish to transition to a lower drop shoe, it is wise to do this in stages.

The stack height is the total height at the heel and at the forefoot (and should include the outsole as well): the difference between the two being the drop. Minimalist shoes have lowest

There is a trend for having thick soles on road shoes. (a) shows a standard road shoe while (b) shows a road shoe with a much thicker sole.

stack height, which essentially means that there is less midsole cushioning between your foot and the road or track. A higher stack height is very valuable for runners with joint problems as additional thickness of foam provides an extra degree of protection from impact.

Rule 7 – Do I need a carbon fibre plate?

Carbon fibre plates have been introduced into the midsoles of shoes to increase the energy return, essentially acting as a spring. Carbon fibre has been the material of choice for amputee athletes because of its physical properties and this has now been translated into plates inserted within the midsole foam of running shoes. This concept was controversially introduced by Nike for their elite athletes but because the participation rules for the Olympics state that only equipment that is available to the general public can be used in the competitions, these shoes have now become more widely available. Initially prices were over £200 but have now come down substantially, although some high-end models are still costing £260 plus.

When running fast, the additional kickback from the plate is noticeable. If you are plodding round at eleven minutes per mile, then you will not notice any difference. Shoes with carbon fibre plates will be stiffer than trainers without plates and may be less comfortable at slower speeds. Other materials such as nylon have been used as cheaper alternatives and offer improved rebound compared to a shoe with no plate.

Rule 8 – Inspect the insole

Check carefully how good the insole is. Sometimes the insoles are very thin and provide little extra comfort, but replacement insoles are widely available, especially thicker versions for longer runs.

Rule 9 – Higher price doesn't automatically mean better

Most brands have shoes at different price points. A higher price doesn't equate to increased shoe comfort. It may just be that the shoes have more unnecessary bells and whistles. Particularly when starting out, get sensibly priced, comfortable shoes. Some of the big sports store chains have their 'own brands' and these appear to perform very creditably. Trail shoes tend to be a little bit more expensive than their road counterparts, as there is extra protective rubber and the midsole and outsoles may be more complex.

Rule 10 – Under- and over-pronation

During the run cycle, the foot will naturally roll inwards very slightly. Some people have excessive inward roll (over-pronators) and some people have less (under-pronators). Once you have been running for a while, the wear pattern on your trainers will tell you which you are. If the wear is on the outside you are an under-pronator. If the wear is all on the inside edge of the shoe you are an over-pronator. Motion control shoes are supposed to control the excessive inward roll (over-pronation), but there is little evidence to suggest they are any better than neutral shoes for mild to moderate over-pronators and the increased stiffness on the inside of the arch may be uncomfortable.

A word on waterproof running shoes

Some manufacturers produce waterproof versions of their running shoes, usually with a Gore-Tex or equivalent waterproof and breathable membrane. This tends to make the upper slightly thicker and stiffer and can affect the fit (you may need a half size larger). These will stop water splashes soaking through into your socks. However, water can still get into the shoes at the heel, and with the membrane, it won't then be able to get out again. They may be more comfortable in winter when you are out running in the rain.

Gaiters

When running trails, there is a tendency for debris such as gravel or pine needles to get into the shoes. This will need to be removed if it is a long race. It is possible to get gaiters that cover the ankle of the shoe and keep the debris out. Some shoe manufacturers make their trail shoes with specific attachment pointers for their gaiters, but third-party gaiters are also available. There are shoes where the tongue is joined to the upper, which will prevent some debris getting in.

A word on laces and lacing

Getting the lacing comfortable is crucial. There are various ways to do this (and lots of helpful videos on YouTube). If you have high arches or flat feet, then changing the lacing may help. Most manufacturers give you two extra eyelets at the ankle: these are so you can create a loop (runner's loop), which holds the ankle more firmly. Elasticated laces with toggles are very comfortable, especially if your feet are going to swell on a long run (also used by triathletes, to save time in transition).

On long runs you may need to adjust the laces. Ensure they are not too tight across the top

Elasticated laces make it much easier to adjust lace tension during long races to account for foot swelling.

of the foot over the metatarsals, as this can be extremely painful and obstructs the blood flow, which will cause additional swelling.

WATERPROOFS

Anyone who runs in the UK is going to spend time out running in rain. Decent waterproofs are an absolutely essential piece of equipment if you are going to take up running seriously, and these will be costly. To be comfortable, jackets will need to be breathable, otherwise the retained sweat will be as bad as the rain. The best products will have a Gore-Tex or equivalent membrane. Check the effective waterproofing and breathability before purchase.

Waterproof and breathable outer layers are more comfortable and function better if you have a layer of clothing between your skin and the outer layer. Otherwise, the waterproofs tend to stick to the skin and impede free movement.

CARE OF RUNNING SHOES

- Try not to use the same shoes every day
- Clean dirt off promptly with water +/- a shoe cleaning foam
- Clean and check insole
- Add water resistance with footwear waterproofer (from outdoor stores)
- Do not wash in machines
- Do not use biological detergents
- Do not tumble dry/dry over radiators (destroys the glues that hold the shoe together)
- Allow to air dry, not in direct sun

EFFECTIVE WATERPROOFING FOR JACKETS AND TROUSERS

6,000–10,000mm	Resists light rain only
11,000–20,000mm	Resists light to moderate rain
>20,000mm	Resists heavy rain

Also check whether the material has a durable water-resistant finish (DWR)

Effective breathability for jackets and trousers:

$<10,000g/m^2$	Not very breathable – suitable for light activity only
$10,000–15,000g/m^2$	Suitable for hill walking
$>15,000g/m^2$	Suitable for running

CARE OF WATERPROOF CLOTHING

- Clean and reproof regularly to maintain waterproofing and breathability
- Wash with specialist detergent (Nikwax or Grangers)
- *Do not* use a biological detergent or conditioner (blocks the holes)
- Rinse with reproofing agent (Nikwax or Grangers)
- Check for areas of wear at site of friction from race packs/waist packs
- Always allow to dry off when wet

KEY FEATURES TO THINK ABOUT WHEN PURCHASING WATERPROOF JACKETS

- What do you intend to use it for (short road run, all day mountain event)?
- How waterproof and breathable is it?
- Check fit (loose enough to allow a layer of air for insulation)
- Will it go over a small waist pack or a race backpack?
- How long is the coat (drop-tail good if you are out in the rain for long periods)?
- How long are the sleeves?
- Velcro or elasticated cuffs
- Thumb holes
- Waterproof zips
- Siting and number of pockets (can you access them easily?)
- Hood (check peak, does it roll up and fasten?)
- Is there a stud at the top to hold the coat open without flapping?
- Taped seams (often specified in mandatory equipment lists)

CLOTHING

There is a huge range of clothing available for runners. The basic requirements are some kind of top, shorts (or skorts), running tights plus appropriate underwear. The key is to make sure that they are comfortable. Look for flatlock seams (to prevent rubbing).

Clothing needs to be appropriate for the weather conditions. Ideally you should be a little cold to start with, but then comfortable when you get warmed up to operating temperature. If

> *'Hi-viz clothing is essential when running in the dark or in gloomy conditions on roads'*

it is going to be a long run and you are starting early, get an idea of the change in temperature that is expected. If you have a race pack you can take off layers and stow them or if the temperature is going to fall, have extra layers to put on.

When running on trails, wearing leggings or running tights can be valuable in preventing injury from bushes or nettles, protecting you from insects such as ticks and will take some of the damage if you fall.

For women it is essential to wear a properly fitted, supportive sports bra to make running much more comfortable. There is evidence that proper sports bras improve running efficiency. Skorts, divided skirts designed for sportswear, can be worn as an alternative to shorts.

Socks require a special mention. These should have reasonable padding on the heel, under the toes and around the front of the toes. Some running socks are very thin on the top of the foot which can cause problems if the laces are too tight and the tongue is also thin: it is important to have some protection on the top of the foot.

Compression clothing such as tops, tights, long shorts and knee-length socks is claimed to improve muscle function and provide support for tired muscles during runs. How much of a difference these items of clothing make to average runners is debatable. There is evidence that the use of compression clothing on the legs after running does make a difference to muscle recovery. To be effective, these need to be very tight and should be quite difficult to get on, and need to fit correctly, so check manufacturers' size recommendations. Look for graded compression. People who suffer from varicose veins may find compression clothing on the legs and ankles reduces the discomfort experienced from the veins. Compression leggings may potentially increase foot swelling over long runs, as they make the venous return slower; knee socks may be better. Compression clothing may have a useful role for runners who are undertaking strength training, again providing support for the muscles through the full range of movement. Be aware that a lot of 'compression clothing' is nothing more than a slightly tighter normal top or bottom, but without proper graded compression.

HI-VIZ CLOTHING

Hi-viz clothing is essential when running in the dark or in gloomy conditions on roads. Clothing that is fluorescent orange or yellow tends to be most visible. Orange is recognised to be the best in terms of visibility. Pink is also used, although I am less convinced that this is adequate. I am not a fan of black winter clothing with additional reflective material. You should not rely on the clothing alone, but use LED armbands, LED reflective Sam Browne belts and head torches to ensure maximum visibility.

RUNNING IN THE DARK

- Wear bright colours, *not* black unless it has a lot of reflective material
- Have clothing/jackets/shoes with reflective material
- Visibility of reflective material is highest when it is on body parts that move most (ankles/wrists/feet)
- Consider reflective or illuminated belt
- Use a good-quality head torch

RACE PACKS AND BUM BAGS

It is useful to have some sort of waist pack or race pack to store stuff while out running. As with shoes, it is vital to try these on in store and check for fit and adjustability.

WATER BOTTLES

You can probably run for an hour without needing to carry replacement fluid unless it is very hot. Beyond that it is wise to have fluid with you. There are lots of different ways of carrying water, so experiment to see what suits you best.

HEAD TORCHES

Head torches are essential for night-time running and for participating in night run competitions which are usually off-road. There is a lot of choice.

SPORTS WATCHES AND NAVIGATION DEVICES

Sports and running GPS watches have become ubiquitous over the last few years and there are models for every price range and activity. To begin with you need a basic GPS watch that will give you time, distance, pace, steps – this won't be too expensive. However, if you're planning on doing running as your preferred exercise, choosing a running-specific watch makes sense. The more expensive models will provide fitness data such as VO_2. The VO_2 data is estimated but it will give you an idea of training status and progress. With additional equipment such as smart insoles, watches can measure power output. The most expensive watches will have complex navigational facilities, the ability to upload planned routes and waypoints and to provide breadcrumb trails if

you're lost, so you can at least find your way back to your start point.

As with head torches, you need to look at the operational time from fully charged and match this to the duration of events you would like to enter. Some watches have light-sensitive screens that will recharge the battery on the run or at least prevent them running down quite so quickly. You can download music onto some watches and some may link to streaming services, or to bank cards for payment on the go. The more expensive models will offer heart rate monitoring (HRM). Chest monitors are generally recognised to be more accurate than wrist-based HRM monitoring.

All the watches use GPS systems: GPS relies on signals from multiple satellites. Most watches are able to log on to any or all of the three main systems: the more systems that the watch can use, the more accurate will be the positional data, but if they are used for actual navigation, extreme caution is required. All watches may struggle to pick up signals in cities with tall buildings, in forests and steep-sided valleys.

Top-end watches may have altimeters, which is useful if running in the mountains. These are usually barometric and may have an ambient temperature monitor and give warning of impending changes to the weather. Less advanced models calculate elevation from your route on a map.

I would strongly advise using screen protectors on your expensive watch. The cost of these is negligible compared to the cost of replacing damaged screens – go for a 9H hardness, as this will be most durable. They are easy to fit and replace. Keep an eye on watch straps, as contact with sweat speeds up their deterioration.

Strava is widely used to track runs. While it can collect data directly via your mobile phone on the run, it may not be accurate and it is usually better to upload data from a dedicated sports watch. Strava enables you to compare your times over routes that other runners use regularly and enables your friends to see how you have got on. One caution though: criminals have been known to study people's public Strava uploads to gain information on times when houses might be empty. Alternatives include MapMyRun and Plot a Route.

RUNNING POLES

Running poles are very useful for trail running in hills and mountains. They enable you to use arm power to assist the legs on steep climbs and help with balance on sheer, rough downhill sections. Poles can take up to 30 per cent of the effort away from the legs. They are valuable when running in snow, with an appropriate basket fitted. There are two main types: telescopic with various locking systems or z-fold. Both types can be adjusted for length. Telescopic poles load more conveniently onto race packs but have a habit of unlocking and collapsing. Z-fold poles are more bulky, and require specific fittings on the race pack, but once extended are locked.

Aluminium, titanium and carbon fibre composites are all used. Carbon fibre tends to be the lightest, strongest and most expensive. Aluminium poles are the cheapest but can bend under extreme force. Titanium is stronger and cheaper than carbon fibre. Leki and Black Diamond are the best-known makers of quality poles, Harrier Run Free and Trail-Running supply very reasonably priced z-fold carbon fibre poles and race packs designed to carry them. When selecting poles, make sure the grips are comfortable and not too slippy (*see* 'Running with poles' in Chapter 6).

OTHER EQUIPMENT

It is helpful to have a whistle in the event of an accident and similarly to have a small torch, both of which can be used with the standard

---

KEY FEATURES TO CHECK WHEN BUYING A SPORTS WATCH

- Know what you will use it for
- Do not pay for features you will never use
- Look at battery life with GPS on and off
- Is heart rate monitoring wrist or chest-strap based?
- How good is the supporting app?
- Check magazine and online reviews and manufacturer information

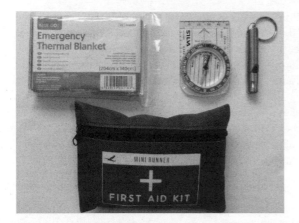

Minimum emergency kit: small First Aid kit, emergency thermal foil blanket, compass and whistle (together with a charged mobile phone).

emergency call (six short blasts followed by a minute's pause and then repeated, although some say three long blasts). Most running-specific race packs include a small whistle. Likewise, if you are going off-road, having maps and a compass are useful provided that you actually know how to use them (*see* 'Navigation', Chapter 4).

It is worth having some simple plasters with you for minor injuries and blisters, but if you are planning on being out for longer, then a small, lightweight first-aid kit is sensible.

Take a mobile phone and make sure it is fully charged. It is wise to install the app What3words on your phone, which will give you a three-word code identifying your position should you need to summon emergency services. Ordnance Survey have an app (OS Locate) which will give your complete grid reference. High-end sports watches will be able to give your full grid reference. It is possible to download mapping apps to your phone, including OS maps, but be aware that they will drain the battery significantly over a long period. Having an additional battery pack may help. For multi-day runs with no access to mains electricity, solar chargers that can hang on the backpack may be a solution.

If you want to listen to music it is better to use bone-conducting headphones so you can hear hazards (cars, bikes, thugs). If you are concerned about your safety, you can buy a small alarm which will attach to keyring/bum bag and when triggered will emit a piercing shriek.

MANDATORY EQUIPMENT

Mandatory kit is not just for organised races but should be considered for any long run, especially if you are running by yourself off-road. For most road races up to marathon, there will be aid stations every few miles, so the need to carry large quantities of food and drink is reduced, unless, like me, you have some very specific requirements. Basic kit will include somewhere to put keys and phone, energy gels or equivalent and some hydration system between aid stations. Depending on the weather it may be helpful to have a lightweight race pack with a thin water/windproof jacket.

Once you start venturing off-road onto trail races, aid stations may be fewer and you may need to carry more supplies. In hot weather you need to ensure that you have enough fluid and in winter enough warm clothing.

> *'Take a mobile phone and make sure it is fully charged'*

Having a first-aid kit and foil blanket is sensible. For longer races in remote countryside, race organisers may well have mandatory kit lists and there may be inspections to ensure that you have the mandated kit. Mandatory kit is for your safety; pay attention to it, it could save your life. Remember as soon as you stop running, unless the weather is very hot, you will start cooling immediately and in winter conditions, hypothermia can set in rapidly. If you are injured and need to be evacuated, you may be out in the elements for some hours.

The following may be included, but you may be wise to take some or all of it anyway even if not mandated. Race organisers may require additional mandatory kit on the day, depending on weather conditions. It pays to take everything and decide what to carry when you get to the venue. This is better than having to either buy or borrow the extra kit or risk disqualification.

Phone: Obviously take your phone and make sure it is fully charged. If the organisers have given you emergency numbers to call, make sure you have these in your phone. Mobile signals may be poor or non-existent, but the emergency call function will link to the emergency services networks which have a wider coverage.

Money/credit card: It is sensible to take some money or a credit card with you in case you get lost and need to get transport back to the start.

Waterproofs: All mandatory kit lists include carrying fully waterproof jackets and trousers and usually specify taped seams (which stop water ingress along seam lines): you can get very lightweight ones from many manufacturers that meet the requirements.

Extra clothing: If the weather is going to be poor or you are going to be climbing high, carry extra warm clothing. Insulated jackets are incredibly light and will usually compress into a tiny bag.

Food and drink: You should have some reserve food (energy bar) and reserve fluid that you do not use during the race.

First-aid kit: You should have a basic first-aid kit. A roll of cohesive bandage that adheres to itself is a worthwhile addition, as you can use it to strap bandages in place and strap a broken leg to a pole or the other leg to stop movement. A triangular bandage is useful.

Foil blanket/rain poncho: Foil blankets are invaluable for insulation and weigh nothing. They do burn however, so keep them away from naked flames. Being light they can be difficult to handle in high winds: make sure they are tucked in and secured. Single-use ponchos are completely waterproof and cover the head as well.

Bivvy bag: Some races insist that you have a proper bivvy bag. These are large orange sacks that you climb in to. They are much more weather-proof than the foil blanket but do weigh more. They are highly visible.

Compass: A compass is essential for navigation, but it is only useful if you know how to use it.

Whistle: A whistle is an absolute requirement in case of emergencies. Many race packs incorporate a whistle into one of the clips.

Torch: A torch may be required for all-day races on the basis that if injured, you may still be out on the mountains after dark. Use the torch to signal in the same way as the whistle.

Map: If the organisers have provided a course map, take it with you and a copy of the relevant area on an OS map. If you can, have these on waterproof paper or stored in a plastic bag. If you have an OS subscription you can download and print the key area. Inkjet printers use water-soluble ink, which will wash away.

Tracker: Some races require you to have a tracker, sometimes supplied by the organisers. These will mostly have an SOS button.

Dry bags: This mandatory kit is going to be no use if it is soaking wet. Invest in dry bags to put your kit in inside your race pack, unless you know that your pack is fully waterproof. Keep the emergency kit in a separate dry bag from the things you need en route, such as gels and drinks.

4 NUTRITION, HYDRATION, SLEEP AND OTHER SKILLS

To train and run effectively, you need to spend time on nutrition, hydration and rest/sleep. You need to develop skills to keep you safe while running, such as a safety-first approach, navigation and first-aid skills.

NUTRITION

This section is not about diets to lose weight, but about how to ensure that you have the right nutrition to run effectively. There is no 'right' diet for running, although there may well be some 'wrong' ones.

Nutrition for runners is difficult. Most of the information is based on measuring grams of carbohydrate, fat and protein, but most of us have little knowledge of how many grams of each will be in our daily meals. Most of us will be making guesses, which may be wildly inaccurate. There is also a significant requirement for vitamins, minerals, trace elements and essential amino acids. Runners, particularly endurance athletes, may have markedly different requirements from sedentary adults. For most runners, an average diet is more than adequate, assuming that it is healthy with a balance of proteins, carbohydrates and healthy fats and a wide range of fruits, vegetables and protein sources. I shall give the current scientific recommendations, recognising that they may not be helpful!

There are some key concepts to cover first. The first issue is how much you weigh and what your BMI (body mass index) is. The BMI is derived from your height and your weight (*see* Resources for details of BMI calculator). There has been criticism of the use of BMI, as it is recognised to be a poor measure of body fat, and does not differentiate between 'good' fat and 'bad' (visceral) fat, but for now it remains a useful measure.

Recent research has suggested that risk of ill-health related to BMI is U-shaped, with the biggest risks of significant health issues in

NHS INTERPRETATION OF BMI	
<18.5	Underweight
18.5–24.9	Healthy
25–29.9	Overweight
30–39.9	Obese
>40	Very obese
Biggest health risks = BMI <20 and >30	

> *'Focusing on getting fit and staying fit is more important for long-term health than achieving an arbitrary target weight'*

those with a BMI of <20 and >30 more likely to be associated with the presence of other illnesses. The implication of this research is that those who are currently healthy and active and fall into the 'overweight' category probably have little to fear, and no pressing need to embark on strenuous (and probably unsuccessful) dieting.

Focusing on getting fit and staying fit is more important for long-term health than achieving an arbitrary target weight. Firstly, muscle weighs more than fat, so increasing muscle size reduces the effect of fat reduction on weight. Body shape changes however, with disappearance of unhealthy fat, typically visceral fat in and around the abdomen. To lose weight, there has to be an extended period when calorie output exceeds calorie input.

HOW MANY CALORIES DO YOU BURN WHEN YOU RUN?

- On average, you will burn 100 calories per mile
- For a 5k run (just over 3 miles) you will burn between 300–400 calories
- The exact figure will depend on the speed/ascent
- A standard-sized Twix has 291 calories!

If running is part of your move to get fit and lose weight, some attention to diet is required, but remember the getting fit itself is the important part. There are some basic rules for diet in relation to running:

1. Eat smaller portions

Most of us eat far bigger portions than we should. The best diet is the 'less food diet'. Reduce portion size slowly. Your stomach expands to match the amount of food you normally eat. When it is empty or incompletely filled it will release the hormone ghrelin which acts on the brain to increase hunger. If you eat less, you will not completely suppress the ghrelin and continue to feel hungry. As you eat less, the stomach gradually shrinks so feels full with less food and the production of ghrelin reduces. Meals with high protein and carbohydrate content suppress ghrelin better than a high-fat meal, so are more effective at suppressing hunger. Sleep deprivation also increases ghrelin levels, increasing hunger, so ensuring good sleep will also help decrease hunger. Another hormone involved is leptin, produced by fat cells when they are filled to capacity, which suppresses hunger. In people who are obese, the brain does not respond as well to the suppressant effects of leptin, so hunger persists leading to inappropriate eating.

You can fool the brain into thinking that the stomach is full by putting the smaller portion on a smaller plate. The plate looks full, which the brain accepts as indicating the correct amount of food. Put the smaller helping onto a large plate and the brain perceives that there is not enough food to satisfy hunger.

2. Avoid fad diets if you are running

To run well and lose weight you need a balanced diet with all the key ingredients. Going onto low-fat, high-protein or other diets may mean that you will no longer get sufficient of the key nutrients that you require to run efficiently.

3. Eat breakfast

Breakfast is the key meal of the day. You have fasted overnight, so the body is waiting for a meal and will utilise food very efficiently. If you don't have breakfast, the body enters starvation mode, where it thinks that there may be a shortage of food and therefore when you do eat, the food is more likely to be converted to fat and sent to storage, in case there is no more food. This is a response that we can thank our hunter-gatherer ancestors for. There is a link between avoiding breakfast and obesity.

4. Have regular meals

As well as having breakfast you need to have other regular meals through the day (at least three). If you are used to having just one meal a day, then you need to divide the total amount of food into three portions, rather than continue to eat one large meal and then add two others. You may need to adjust the timing so that you do not run on a full stomach.

5. Avoid highly processed foods

Highly processed foods have high levels of sugar, fat and salt and may have inadequate protein and be missing key vitamins, minerals, trace elements and essential amino acids. High-fat foods do not suppress ghrelin effectively and therefore leave you hungry. Freshly cooked meat, fish, vegetables, nuts, legumes, seeds or fruit are far healthier and will contain the correct balance of nutrients. Avoid hydrogenated fats (trans fats) and have more polyunsaturated fats (fish oil, vegetable oils). Remove excess fat from meat before cooking.

6. Calorie requirements

Calculating how many calories you require each day and the extra for runs is governed by complex formulae. We all have a basic calorie requirement, which covers the body's energy requirement for general activities and the normal functioning of organs. Additional calories will be required for activity above the baseline (*see* Resources for online calculator

details). The apps with some sports watches will calculate your basal and active calories. On average you need 100 calories per mile, so tot up the total miles per week, multiply by 100 and divide by seven to get your average daily requirement, on top of your baseline. It is estimated that women should have 1,940 calories per day and men 2,550. If you are trying to lose weight, reduce the calories by about 15 per cent from the calculated level. During a race you probably need to consume 100–300 calories per hour. It is important to ensure that the calorie intake is adequate for the level of activity.

7. Carbohydrate

The volume of carbohydrate that runners require will vary according to the level of physical activity. For average activity (low volume/intensity) 3–5g/kg/day, this increases up to 6–10g/kg/day for high volume/intensity. For carb-loading immediately before a race, the requirement may be up to 12g/kg/day. Not all carbohydrates are born equal. Foods can be assessed on their glycemic index, which is a related to how high the blood glucose goes after a meal. Free sugars (glucose, fructose, sucrose, lactose) and quickly digested foods (potato, white bread, bananas) all have high glycemic indices, whereas foods from which sugars are released slowly by digestion (beans, nuts) have lower GIs – they are essentially slow-release forms of carbohydrate. Slow-release carbohydrate does have advantages for running in that it encourages the burning of fat.

8. Fat

Fat is an important energy source for running, as it has a very high energy density. Cutting down fat intake is important where weight loss is a major goal, but ultra-low-fat diets tend to cause poor running performance. Replacing fat with carbohydrate is unhelpful. Fat in the diet is also important for the uptake of fat-soluble vitamins (vitamins A, D, E, K) and other micronutrients. Omega-3 and omega-6 fatty acids are particularly important and are obtained from oily fish, nuts and seeds, soybeans, eggs, nuts and avocado, while saturated fats (animal fat) should be reduced; 20–35 per cent of calories should come from fat, divided between monounsaturated, polyunsaturated and saturated fat. Science now suggests that margarines and similar spreads (processed) may be worse than butter (natural fat).

9. Protein

Protein intake is required for building and repairing all parts of the body, but especially muscles. Intake for sedentary adults is estimated at 0.8g/kg/day. Recreational endurance athletes require between 1–1.2g/kg/day, but competitive endurance athletes may require up to 2g/kg/day. Ingested protein is broken down to its constituent amino acids and then resynthesized into whatever proteins the body requires. Whey protein from milk is an excellent source of essential amino acids and therefore milk or drinks derived from whey protein make excellent recovery drinks post-exercise.

Vitamins, minerals and supplements

In addition to the three main components of the diet, the body also requires vitamins and minerals (micronutrients). Runners may have higher needs but provided that runners are having a balanced diet with plenty of vegetables, it is likely they will be getting enough of the key micronutrients. Many runners also take a daily supplement. For most vitamins and minerals there are recommended daily allowances (RDAs), which should be stated on the packaging for the supplement. Iron, magnesium, calcium, and zinc are all required and there is increasing focus on the roles that antioxidants play in maintaining health and moderating tissue damage (including muscle damage caused

by running). A broadly based diet should be adequate to supply all these requirements but some groups may be at risk of deficiencies, for example menstruation can cause iron deficiency, and vegan runners may lack some micronutrients in their diet.

There is no good evidence that mega-dose vitamins help performance. For a lot of supplements, it is the placebo effect that helps. Provided that there is no harm, then it doesn't matter whether it is a real or placebo effect.

Creatine is a widely used supplement, said to help build muscle strength and for energy production. It is not considered to be illegal by the World Anti-doping Agency (WADA). Lots of studies have shown improvement in exercise performance and prevention/reduction of injuries. There has been concern that creatine can cause kidney problems; anyone with known kidney disease should check with their GP before starting it.

Nutrition for training

To train effectively it is crucial to get nutrition right. This needs to take into account any weight loss targets, but you will not be able to run effectively if you do not have enough calories, protein and micronutrients. The more you progress and the harder you are running, the more important this becomes. If your performance is not what you are expecting, or has deteriorated, as well

'Supplements do not provide a shortcut to better/faster running that avoids proper training'

as looking at your training plan, you should also review nutrition and hydration.

After a run, the hunger hormone ghrelin is high as the stomach is empty and leptin is increased as fat has been mobilised. Eating reverses this. If you do not eat enough after a run, leptin remains high and this encourages the body to conserve energy and store fat, so having some food with enough energy to replace what you have used is wise. The body stores about 1,200–1,600 calories of carbohydrate as glycogen, enough to run for 60–90 minutes or up to two hours at slower paces. Very intense training sessions will exhaust the glycogen in 45 minutes or less. However, the brain and nervous system absolutely must have glucose for fuel, so there should be adequate carbohydrate intake to replace it. If glycogen stores are exhausted, it will take 24 hours for them to be completely replenished. Failure to fully replace glycogen stores due to inadequate intake of carbohydrate while continuing to exercise will lead to a gradual deterioration of performance.

There was a vogue for training while fasted, that is running first thing in the morning after an overnight fast. The rationale was that this improved muscle fat burning. More recent studies have shown no evidence that this approach has any training benefit and reduces the capacity to train at high intensity, so it is probably best avoided. Likewise, low carbohydrate/high fat diets had no benefit.

Provided that you are having a balanced diet, taking an additional protein supplement is not required, even though your protein requirements will be greater than a sedentary person. Very high protein diets will stress the kidneys, as the unwanted nitrogen derived from the excess protein has to be excreted.

The amount of salt you lose through sweating is highly variable and will change according to temperature and training status. The amount of salt in electrolyte drinks may not be enough to keep up and therefore you may need to consider additional salty snacks after a run. If it is a long run, in hot weather, carry salt tablets. There is a fashion for using coconut water on the basis that this is a 'better' rehydration fluid, but its salt content is less than for commercial rehydration fluids or more specific running hydration powders.

The takeaway messages for post-training eating are: get some carbohydrate in quickly after the run and eat a balanced diet with plenty of carbohydrate, fat and protein; if you are aiming for weight loss, don't cut out any key nutrients, just have smaller portions; if you are persistently tired after exercise, look at your calorie intake – are you failing to replace what you have used?

It is extremely important to practise your race day nutrition during training. This involves not only testing out different types of foods, but also working out how much you need to keep going, especially if planning to do races over 90 minutes, the average time your glycogen stores will last. Work out your schedule for fuelling starting with immediately pre-training, during the run and replenishment of stores after training.

Just as your actual training needs to be periodised, with peaks and troughs (recovery), so your nutrition needs to be adjusted accordingly. Injury always causes a problem, as the loss of exercise affects your mental state and this can lead to eating junk food as 'compensation', which obviously makes matters a lot worse in the longer term. If you are injured, adjust the diet sooner rather than later.

Vegan running

Eating a good vegan diet is entirely compatible with high performance running, provided that certain precautions are taken. Some substances present in plants reduce the absorption of proteins, and it is important to have a broad range of protein sources. The body cannot manufacture some amino acids, so they are absolutely required in the diet, essential for building, maintaining and repairing muscle. Supplements may be advisable where training or racing is intense. Vegetable-based fats (polyunsaturates) are far healthier than meat-based fats.

Vegan diets can be deficient in vitamin B12. This can be found in some vegetable products but levels tend to be quite low. A supplement may be wise. Vitamin D can also be deficient in vegan diets, although being outside running helps the body make its own, as long as skin is exposed and there is sunshine. A balance must be struck between avoiding UV-triggered skin damage and healthy sun exposure. Vitamin D is responsible for bone strength, but also controls calcium absorption. Calcium is important for muscle function. Iodine may be deficient in vegan diets which can lead to an underactive thyroid and swelling of the gland. An underactive thyroid gland will contribute to poor performance with fatigue and weight gain as major features. Although there is plenty of iron in a plant-based diet, the absorption is reduced by plant tannins, especially tea. Iron absorption can be enhanced by vitamin C. Zinc deficiency can also occur, and this can make iron deficiency worse.

If you are on a vegan diet and doing a lot of running, an annual blood check for key nutrients is wise.

Nutrition pre-race

Nutrition before running/racing tends to be an individual thing and you need to work out what foods suit you best. Magazines such as *Runner's World* and *Trail Running* have plenty of advice on foods to try. You need to leave at least an hour and preferably longer (up to three hours) after a large meal.

The question of what to eat is controversial. We have been through the phase of carb-loading pre-race, with pre-race pasta parties, but the evidence of benefit is scant: the body is only capable of storing so much glycogen, the immediate-use energy store for the muscle. However, it makes sense to ensure a high-carbohydrate intake in the days leading up to the race. Most of the energy for longer runs comes from muscle switching from burning glucose to burning fat. For all but the elite, eating your normal diet is most sensible, as changes to the diet before a race are likely to cause more problems than benefits.

The best advice is to avoid high fibre/high residue diets in the 24 hours before a race or very long runs. However, there are plenty of runners for whom a full English breakfast an hour before a run/race is standard fare and seems to cause them no problems. Having a mix of simple sugars and complex carbohydrate is sensible, perhaps porridge or toast with butter and peanut butter.

It has been suggested that using probiotics reduces the risks of gastrointestinal upsets during races, so if you are prone to such problems then this may be worth a try in the run-up to races.

'If you are on a vegan diet and doing a lot of running, an annual blood check for key nutrients is wise'

Which foods improve performance?

- Caffeine is the most obvious stand-out performance-improving food. There is clear evidence of improvement in muscle function after caffeine. It improves the efficiency of burning glucose and helps restore glycogen after exercise. It is entirely legal, removed from the list of banned substances by the World Anti-Doping Agency in 2004. How much you need is open to question.

Caffeine is a diuretic and too much will also cause palpitations, dizziness, nausea and a wired feeling. Gels and drinks can have between 30–150mg of caffeine. The amount of caffeine in coffee varies hugely. Caffeine tablets are available, but I would not recommend these. Tea has similar compounds to caffeine (theobromine) which will have similar effects. Caffeine and theobromine are both good for dilating the airways, so asthmatic runners may find a coffee before running helpful.

- Dark chocolate contains caffeine and epicatechin, which increases the production of nitric oxide in the body. Nitric oxide improves endurance.
- Beetroot juice contains high levels of nitrates, which have a similar effect to chocolate, and there is solid scientific evidence of a performance benefit from having beetroot juice several hours before exercise (if you can stand the flavour!). Other sources of nitrates are rocket and spinach.
- Calcium and magnesium are essential for optimum muscle function, but on a normal diet you should have plenty of these without supplements. Some sports electrolyte drinks do contain small amounts of calcium and magnesium. Beware of taking magnesium supplements before races; magnesium salts are laxatives (Epsom salts) and will cause diarrhoea.
- Plant anthocyanins are useful antioxidants, as is vitamin C and these can reduce inflammation and tissue damage. A good diet with plenty of coloured fruits and vegetables will supply your needs.
- Fish oils have antioxidant and anti-inflammatory effects so are beneficial.
- Turmeric is helpful for reducing joint pain and is an anti-inflammatory.
- Beta-alanine (an amino acid) is recognised as beneficial for exercise. Taking a beta-alanine supplement before exercise can support higher intensity for longer. SIS do a gel containing caffeine and beta-alanine.
- Sodium bicarbonate improves exercise tolerance. However, it is very difficult to know how much to take and side effects (gastric upset and diarrhoea) mean that it should *not* be used except under professional supervision.

Nutrition during races

Nutrition during races up to an hour in duration is probably not necessary, provided that you have trained effectively and your muscles can burn fat. Having a sports gel with caffeine before the start may provide a boost, or a coffee and a flapjack or banana, but allow time to digest. For running up to a half-marathon, you can aim to have one gel per hour. Jelly babies are a useful and well-tolerated source of energy. Avoid having too many sports gels as they can make you feel sick. Gels come in a variety of flavours, with or without caffeine. If you don't like the gels, Clif Shot blocks are an alternative.

The downside of topping up with sugary foods is that as they wear off, you can get more fatigued and they reduce the fat burning. You should probably aim for about 30–60g carbohydrate per hour for the first three hours. A banana is roughly 25g carbohydrate. For runs beyond three hours, increase to 60–90g per hour. Having the carbohydrate with caffeine during the run will be helpful.

One caution about topping up with sugar: If you have been running for a long while and guzzle a lot of sugar in one go, this will lead to

---

THE GOLDEN RULE FOR RACE DAY NUTRITION IS

- No new foods that you have not tested out in training
- This applies to tasty treats at aid stations
- Forget this at your peril

For longer runs there is a wide variety of pre-prepared gels and bars, or you can make your own energy bars.

a sudden peak in insulin secretion, especially if the blood sugar has been lowered by impending exhaustion of the glycogen stores. This can lead to a sharp drop in the blood sugar and make you feel dizzy. Take sugar in small quantities, do this regularly throughout your run/race and try to have some complex carbohydrates as well (maltodextrin, starchy foods) which act as the slow-release glucose and will stop or reduce fluctuations in blood sugar.

Once you get to marathons or longer, you need to consider having proper food including protein to keep you going. Aid stations may have food, which is great. Hopefully the organisers will give information on what will be offered, so you can plan what to take. You can prepare your own energy bars; there are lots of recipes on the internet with healthy ideas (see Resources).

Your taste buds will be pretty shot, so you need something with a lot of flavour. My coach recommended cheese and pickle sandwiches, or try peanut butter or avocado. Other sources of complex slowly digested carbohydrate used by ultrarunners include cold boiled salted potatoes, noodles and salted nuts. Be cautious in how much you eat. For all foods that you eat en route, be sure that you have practised eating them on long runs before the big day: do not try something from the aid station just because it looks nice. I like a high-caffeine gel to get me through the last hour of a race. Caffeine has been shown to reduce fatigue and the perception of exertion.

Over long races, calculate how much you need to take and stick to the plan, so you don't run out in the later stages: use the aid stations for top-up, but don't rely on them. If you are towards the back (my accustomed place) the faster vultures may have swept the tables clear.

The main cause of 'hitting the wall' (aka 'bonking') in longer races is running out of fuel and fluid. This usually occurs when your body's stores of glycogen have been exhausted and the blood sugar starts to drop. Training for endurance encourages your muscles to burn more fat and less glycogen (glucose). Training also needs to encompass learning how to fuel on the run and working out what foods suit you best. Eating small amounts regularly throughout is the best strategy, as the digestive system will not be working efficiently during a race. Also ensure that you are drinking plenty of fluid. Hitting the wall causes fatigue and negative feelings, amplifies muscle aches and pains and can cause quite significant disorientation and difficulty in thinking (the brain *really* needs glucose to function). Try to get quick-acting carbohydrate on board and use mental imagery and distraction techniques to get you through.

Be prepared to walk for a bit while you get sorted. If you are not improving, then be prepared to drop out as continuing may lead to collapse and the need for medical assistance.

Nutrition in recovery

Recovery after a run or race requires attention to nutrition. There will be damage to

> *'Try and get quick-acting carbohydrate on board and use mental imagery and distraction techniques to get you through'*

DEALING WITH IN-RACE BOWEL PROBLEMS (DIARRHOEA, CRAMPS, URGENCY OF EVACUATION)

- The bowel becomes relatively ischaemic during long runs as blood is diverted to the muscles. Digestion is therefore poor
- Avoid high-fibre foods before and during races
- Restrict gels to hourly
- Stick to maximum fluid intake per hour
- Compression stockings have been shown to reduce symptoms possibly by increasing bowel blood flow

muscle fibres which the body must repair, and energy stores need to be replaced. In the 90 minutes immediately after a run/race, the body takes up carbohydrate extremely readily and converts it to glycogen to replenish the liver and muscle stores. If you depleted your stores during a longer run, you will need to have plenty of carbohydrate in the post-race period.

Your body also needs protein to repair and rebuild muscles. Milky drinks are a good and easily digestible source of protein, some fat and milk sugar (lactose). BCAA (branch-chain amino acids) supplements may help speed up recovery. You can buy specific recovery drinks or powders which will replace most of what you need and have the advantage of replacing fluid and being relatively easy to digest. Hunger and thirst after a run/race can be confused by the brain, so remember that you need to replace all the fluid and salts lost. However, if you can get a proper meal in the two hours after a run, that is the best way. Running magazines and the internet are awash with meal suggestions for the post-race period.

As well as its benefits before and during races, caffeine immediately after exercise improves muscle glycogen re-synthesis, which in turn helps the muscles recover faster.

Nutrition during injury or illness

If you are injured or ill and unable to run, you need to look carefully at your diet. Recovery from injury requires energy and protein; you may need extra protein to repair or rebuild muscle, in particular sources of BCAA. Likewise repair or coping with illness requires calories, so avoiding carbohydrate is unwise. Increasing the intake of turmeric and omega-3 fish oils will both reduce inflammation. If you are unable to run for a prolonged period, reduce your calorie intake to avoid excessive weight gain.

Irritable bowel syndrome

Irritable bowel syndrome (IBS) is a very common problem. Typical symptoms include constipation, diarrhoea, urgency of evacuation, stomach cramps, bloating and fatigue. If you have developed these symptoms recently, before assuming that they are due to IBS you should check them out with your doctor, who may recommend some investigations to rule out inflammatory bowel or coeliac disease.

The cause of IBS is not known for certain. Many sufferers are aware that certain foods will set off symptoms. While it is not considered to be a typical food allergy, there is some evidence that the immune system is involved. It is also thought that the range and type of bacteria that live in the bowel may also contribute, although this is difficult to analyse as changing diet also affects the bacterial flora. Most people with IBS are aware that stress and anxiety will make symptoms much worse, indicating that there is a direct link between brain and bowel. At the moment treatment is mostly symptomatic, directed towards relieving symptoms such as cramps, diarrhoea and constipation. Dieticians may also recommend changes to the diet.

Wheat is often blamed and some people with IBS do find improvement in their symptoms if they avoid wheat. A wheat-free diet is not quite the same as a gluten-free diet. There is also interest in foods rich in FODMAPS (fermentable oligosaccharides, disaccharides, monosaccharides and polyols) as a cause of symptoms. These substances are widely found in vegetable-based foods. Runners with IBS need to be cautious about their pre-race nutrition and select carefully. Glucose/sucrose-based energy drinks/gels are best.

Remember to experiment with drinks and food during training runs, not during races.

The use of probiotics may help reduce in-race gastrointestinal problems.

RED-S

RED-S stands for relative energy deficiency in sport. As the name suggests, it is due to an imbalance between the energy intake in food and energy expended during sports. Basically, RED-S means not eating enough to cope with the energy required for maintenance of normal bodily functions and exercise on top. Some of these symptoms overlap with the overtraining syndrome and there are links to formal eating disorders such as anorexia and bulimia.

Recognition is the key, either by the runner or by coaches. Standardised questionnaires are available for screening. Management is complex and requires input from a range of specialists. Running should cease until there has been a full investigation and a plan for treatment initiated. If you think you might fall into this category, please see your GP sooner rather than later.

HYDRATION

Hydration during training

Even when training you need to consider proper hydration and carry appropriate fluids. Training is the time to experiment with

> ### 'Training is the time to experiment with replacement fluids and find what works best'

recommendations for rehydration solutions, comprises: 480ml water or coconut water, ½ teaspoon sea salt, 4 tsp white granulated sugar or honey and a squeezed large slice of lemon or lime. You can change the flavours if you like but you need to stick to the same amount of water, salt and sugar. If you add more sugar, you will actually slow or stop the absorption of the water.

replacement fluids and find what works best. It is also the opportunity to practise carrying your own fluids in whatever form you have chosen and make sure it is comfortable.

For very short runs (5k or less) there is no requirement to carry fluid. For runs between 5–10k or under an hour, unless it is very hot or you know that you sweat a lot, there is no real requirement to carry fluid but if you do, then water alone or a plain electrolyte solution is usually sufficient. Beyond an hour in training, consider taking some fluid with you, for which an electrolyte solution is probably best (with or without carbohydrate and caffeine). Although previously advice was given on specific amounts to drink per hour, it is now considered best to drink to thirst to avoid under or over hydration, as individuals' requirements vary widely. The rough range will be 300–800ml per hour, but the gut cannot process much more than 800–1,200ml per hour. If going on a very long run either carry extra or drop off supplies at points along the route before you set off.

Many different varieties of fluid replacement are available, with or without caffeine. If you have a drink with carbohydrate, check which sugar is used: fructose in large quantities may cause stomach cramps and diarrhoea in people with intolerance, especially those with IBS.

- **Making your own drink.** A basic DIY sports drink, based on WHO

Fluid is best sipped frequently in small quantities, rather than infrequent large amounts, to maximise absorption and avoid large quantities of unabsorbed fluid sloshing about in your stomach. As you train, your body will learn to sweat more to control body temperature, meaning that fit runners may need more fluid and electrolytes.

While current advice is to drink to thirst, by the time you feel thirsty, you may already have lost up to 2 per cent of bodyweight as fluid and this level will already be impairing performance. Trying to catch up this loss can be difficult, especially in a race setting. Very highly trained ultrarunners may well tolerate this level of dehydration without impairment of performance, but this requires training and has risks (especially kidney failure). Getting into the habit of drinking regularly through longer runs and races is the best strategy. Be aware that sensation of thirst may decline as you get older, so older runners need to be even more careful. Feeling tired towards the end of long runs may be as much due to lack of fluid as lack of food.

A word of caution: if you are using sugary drinks very regularly and consuming gels/ sweets with sugar, you increase your risk of dental damage. Ideally swallow the drink straight down, to minimise contact with the teeth. Problems are magnified if you add a lot of squeezed lemon juice, as this is acidic and will damage tooth enamel. When you get home, clean your teeth with a fluoride toothpaste or use a fluoride mouthwash.

Hydration during and after races

Hydration for races should be the same as during training, unless weather conditions are extremely adverse. For short races up to an hour you will not normally need much additional fluid. After an hour you need to have a rehydration strategy. The key is to sip regularly. It is important to have a system where you can easily see how much you are drinking and getting used to rationing this out is useful and should be practised in training.

What you should drink is debated. If you sweat a lot, you will lose salt as well as water, and this can cause performance problems. Salt loss is quite variable and trained endurance runners often lose more than average runners. As well as salt, many drinks also contain small amounts of calcium and magnesium, which help with muscle function. Drinking excessive amounts of water alone over a long period can lead to low blood sodium which is dangerous (*see* Chapter 9).

Sipping small amounts regularly through the run is the best way of ensuring tolerability and maximising your chances of avoiding serious

> *'Sipping small amounts regularly through the run is the best way of ensuring tolerability and maximising your chances of avoiding serious dehydration'*

KEY HYDRATION TIPS

- No need for fluids up to one hour in cool conditions
- Above one hour, sip steadily
- Use sports electrolyte drink
- Do not drink huge volumes of water alone
- Check whether carbohydrate is fructose or glucose/sucrose
- Decide whether you want a drink with caffeine
- If very hot, consider extra salt tablets
- Normal requirement is 300–800ml/hr depending on temperature
- Gut maximum absorption during exercise is 800–1,200ml/hr
- In races, make sure you carry enough fluid to cope if aid stations have run out

dehydration. In very hot weather, increase your intake appropriately. If you know you are likely to be running in the heat, training in the heat beforehand will help and will give you an idea of how much fluid and salt you will need to maintain hydration for good performance.

If you are planning an endurance race and know that there will be aid stations with water available, it may be more convenient to carry powder sachets of your electrolyte drink. There is a slight risk if you are towards the back of the pack that the aid stations may run out of water (it does happen!), so it is best not to be 100 per cent reliant on this strategy. On hot days, runners often use the drinking water to pour over their heads, as well as drinking it. While understandable, it is rather selfish. If you are running trail races, dipping your cap in a clean stream or splashing your head will help.

You will continue to sweat after stopping exercise and so the recommended fluid replacement is 1.25–1.5× the estimated loss. Weighing yourself when normally hydrated and then weighing yourself after an event will give you an idea of the requirement; 1l water weighs 1kg. Any post-race weight change is almost entirely down to fluid loss.

SLEEP

Sleep hygiene

Sleep is crucial to good running performance. Average adults require six to eight hours of good-quality sleep, but some people get by on much less and others need more to thrive. Exercise on the whole promotes sleep, but it is unwise to exercise less than two hours before bedtime, as this will have an alerting effect. Many running watches will monitor sleep and give you an idea of your sleep pattern. Sleep is disturbed by intense activity: you may be tired after a long run or race but still have disturbed sleep. Sore muscles after exertion may also contribute to sleep disturbance: legs may be very restless and jumpy after extreme exertion. Inadequate sleep will contribute to poor recovery after training, lead to hormonal abnormalities and negatively affect the immune system.

Ensuring adequate sleep before races is important. If the race is a long way away, arranging accommodation close to the event beforehand and afterwards is wise to avoid a very early start. If travelling abroad for races, bear in mind time difference and the impact of jet lag.

Sleep deprivation

For continuous multi-day/night events, sleep deprivation can be a significant issue. Sleep deprivation increases the perception of effort, impairs cognitive function and affects temperature control. Caffeine will override the effect in the short-term only. Most of the extreme ultra runners have systems in place to have rest stops at aid stations where they can have short sleeps before continuing.

At a lower level, if you are sleep deprived in your daily life for whatever reason your running performance will suffer. The good news is that running and other types of exercise will generally improve sleep.

OTHER SKILLS

As well as paying attention to nutrition, hydration and sleep, it is important when training and racing to develop other skills, particularly in regard to safety, navigation and first aid and to consider whether getting specific insurance is wise, for example if you are injured and unable to work.

Safety

Running does have its dangers and it is important to take steps to minimise these. These days the most important piece of safety equipment is a mobile phone, but keep it out of sight (and charged). If running alone, take care to avoid obvious trouble spots and consider carrying a safety alarm. In some places heckling and abuse of runners, particularly women, is commonplace. Try to run with friends rather than alone. If running at night, avoid unlit areas if possible.

'These days the most important piece of safety equipment is a mobile phone, but keep it out of sight'

Daytime running

Running during the day is obviously less hazardous than running during darkness. If running on roads with no pavements, the advice is that you should run on the right-hand side of the road (in the UK), facing oncoming traffic. If you are running with a large group then the group should run on the left-hand side. If there is a pavement and it is in suitable condition, you should use it. Even in good light during daytime it is important to consider your clothing selection so that you remain highly visible to road traffic.

Many people like to run listening to music with headphones on, so may not hear vehicles approaching. For road races run under England Athletics permits, headphones are banned and only bone-conducting earphones are permitted.

Night-time running

The same rules for road use apply at night as during the day, however it is essential to wear highly visible and preferably reflective clothing. Even if you are planning on running entirely on pavements in built-up areas where there is streetlighting, it is still advisable to wear highly visible clothing. Fluorescent yellow or orange are best; orange is deemed to be more visible than yellow. Usually when running in the dark, it is going to be in the winter and having a waterproof, breathable hi-viz jacket is a useful addition to the running wardrobe. Beanies and gloves with reflective features are also useful.

It is easier for drivers to see light bouncing off moving reflective material so it is more important to have it on the legs, feet and arms.

If running in unlit areas, wearing a head torch is advisable. Firstly, a head torch will help you see the path ahead and identify any hazards or other people in good time and secondly, you can also be more easily seen by others. If you're running in a group, remember not to look straight at one of your colleagues with the head torch on main beam as this will affect their vision for some time. It is also advisable to have red flashing lights either on an arm band or waistband. If wearing a single armband, make sure it is on the outside arm.

Trail running

The main hazards for trail running are obviously trip and fall hazards. Many trails will be uneven with protruding rocks and tree roots and excavations by animals such as badgers and rabbits. On well-used rocky paths, the rocks become polished through the passage of many feet. This means that they become very slippery when wet. Downhill tracks with lots of loose stones and gravel can also be quite unstable. One of the advantages of trail running is that you have to be much lighter on your feet with good balance. When running on trails you need to keep looking ahead, not just at your feet, to spot hazards and take action in good time. Do not follow too close to the runner in front as you will not see hazards until too late.

It is important to have footwear that is appropriate, with a highly durable outsole. The best outsole material is Vibram, but other manufacturers have developed outsole rubber specifically for trail use. Manufacturers make different types of shoes for soft, flat trails, muddy trails and rocky trails.

The main safety issue for off-road running is navigation. It is particularly important when running in hilly or mountainous areas where the weather may change suddenly to have a clearly planned route and to have identified in advance potential escape routes if there are problems. If you're going out alone, leave information about your proposed route and expected return time with appropriate people. If you do this, it is unwise to suddenly change your route unless it is necessary for safety reasons. If you are likely to get back later than anticipated, try to let the people holding your route know. Always make sure that you let people know when you are back safely. Search and rescue teams regularly get called out only to find that the 'missing' person has returned and is currently safe in the local pub.

> ## 'Be aware if running in open country about hazards from farm animals, especially if you are running with your dog'

Be extremely careful about running with a dog through fields with cows, especially if they have calves, as they will be very protective. If necessary, let go of the dog – this will hopefully distract the cows. Never get between a cow and its calf. Even sheep can cause injury – some mountain sheep with lambs may be very protective. If you are running with your dog, make sure that it is under close control in fields with stock. Farmers are entitled to shoot dogs that attack their sheep and will usually do so without hesitation. It is worth checking routes carefully in advance, and if necessary, doing a reconnaissance run without the dog first to assess suitability. Of course, farmers move stock around so look for suitable detours if you are concerned.

If you are running in hills and mountains, always consider the safety of the route, especially if the weather is bad. Be cautious about narrow rocky paths with sheer drops on either side, especially when the rocks are wet. Even experienced mountain runners fall off such paths and suffer serious injuries. The basic rule is that if it looks dangerous, it is! If you are unsure, turn back or choose a different or safer route. It is essential when running off-road to concentrate and be continuously aware of potential hazards.

Falls, bruises and other minor injuries are much more likely while out trail running and it makes sense to carry a small first-aid kit. The online store Harrier Run Free does runner-bespoke kits.

Be aware that many locations may have minimal or no mobile phone signal and while it is important to take a mobile phone which is fully charged, you may only be able to get an emergency signal. If you're planning a long run in a remote area it may be worth hiring a GPS-based geo-locator.

There are various night-time trail runs and clearly it is essential for these to have a suitable head torch together with spare batteries or a spare torch. These should be fully charged before the event. Organised long-distance races will often have a mandatory kit list (*see* Chapter 3).

Weather
When running for longer periods or in hilly/ mountainous areas it is important to check the weather and make allowances for the effect of your intended climb and possible windchill on your selection of equipment and clothing. The UK national parks usually have up-to-date information about weather conditions on their websites. Be aware that conditions in mountainous areas can change rapidly and be very localised.

KEY NAVIGATION TIPS

- Plan the route beforehand
- Use route cards
- Tell someone where you are going
- Know how to use a map and compass (get training)
- Download and print maps on waterproof paper
- Don't rely on a phone for navigation (save power for emergencies)
- Upload GPX files to watch if you can
- Have OS Locate app or What3Words app on your phone
- For runs in remote areas consider a GPS tracker

Navigation

There is no doubt that some people are better at navigating than others. If you are somebody who struggles with navigation, it is wise when going out for runs to have a planned route with key waypoints identified. Write the waypoints down on a card (use waterproof ink!) or even your arm. If your navigation is poor, make sure that you carry some cash or a card with you so that you can get public transport or a taxi back to your start point if you get lost.

In urban environments Google Maps is very useful, however in the rural areas it can be unhelpful or even frankly misleading. If you are running in anything other than organised events it is sensible to carry a map of the area. In the UK the best maps are produced by Ordnance Survey. They have apps for mobile phones so that you can download appropriate maps (a subscription is required). You can log on through your computer and print off maps of specific areas. You can buy waterproof A4 paper for laser printers. Harvey produce excellent maps of National Parks which are available in a waterproof format, and key area maps in conjunction with the British Mountaineering Club (BMC), which are strong, lightweight and waterproof. The Harvey maps may be slightly easier to read when looking for footpaths and so on. Be aware that footpaths on the ground may not follow exactly the route specified on the map, and people have been known to alter or remove signs. Some trail races may use tracks on private land where access is given specifically for the race so please do not abuse this by trying to use the tracks at other times.

When out in the countryside, follow the Countryside Code. In particular, pay attention to leaving gates as you found them, and do not block access to farmer's fields. Nothing annoys farmers more than having to spend hours rounding up their sheep which have escaped because a gate was not closed.

You should be familiar with reading maps and with the use of a compass. Key aspects to learn are how to find and give a grid reference

for your location. The first is the grid letters of the 100km square, this is then followed by the Easting (read off the horizontal axis of the map) and the Northing (read off the vertical axis). The axes of the map have the numbers and then you have to estimate the intermediate points. You should also be able to recognise the symbols for roads, bridleways and footpaths and the contours, which tell you how high the land is above sea-level. Contours that are close together = very steep. You also need to recognise the symbols for the different terrains, especially cliff edges and bogs. It is worth being

> ## 'Remember: if you open a gate, make sure you shut it again'

able to recognise landmarks such as railways, power lines, buildings, as well as useful things like loos, car parks and pubs. Every map has the key to the symbols on the side. Learn how to use a compass to take bearings and identify where you are the old-fashioned way. I recommend *Map and Compass: A comprehensive guide to navigation* by Pete Hawkins (*see* Further Reading). If you are using a map for navigation, write down a route card giving the waypoints with identifying features and keep this accessible.

The more expensive option here is to buy a GPS-based navigation device. Garmin do reasonably lightweight devices. You buy the maps on microSD cards, and Garmin have global coverage if you are planning on travelling outside of the UK. The more expensive GPS running watches also have map facilities. Some of the cheaper ones will simply have a breadcrumb trail to retrace your steps to your start point, others will display a real-time map. The disadvantage of this is that the watch screen is quite tiny. You can usually produce a file of proposed routes as GPX files, which can be uploaded to the watch. It is still sensible to have a route card in case your watch fails.

The bottom line is that all electronic devices can fail and batteries can go flat. The devices are dependent on being able to get good GPS signals from satellites. It is essential that you have the manual back-up system, the ability to navigate with a map and compass – get out into the field and practise this for real. There are many organisations that offer navigation

training and if you're planning self-supported runs then it makes sense to know what you're doing.

If you need to summon assistance from the emergency services, dial 999 and if you are in the mountains, ask for mountain rescue. You may need to use the emergency function on your mobile phone: this connects to the emergency services network and will work sometimes when there is no signal from your normal provider. You will need to be able to identify exactly where you are. GPS watches will be able to give you your co-ordinates. If you have a hardcopy map then you should be able to read off your grid reference, assuming that you know exactly where you are. Having given them the location do not move without letting the emergency services know, so the time is not wasted looking in the wrong place. Ordnance Survey's OS Locate App is an alternative and will give the full grid reference. There may be areas where this facility is not available so if you plan on visiting these, getting a satellite-based emergency system is sensible.

You can also register your phone with Emergency SMS, originally designed for the deaf and speech impaired, but works well in areas where the mobile signal is weak or battery power is low. Search and rescue teams also use SARLOC (Search and Rescue Location). The rescue team sends a text message with a link which when clicked will send them your location.

If you want to track your location or allow someone else to, there are a number of options. Some races have trackers as a mandatory requirement and will supply them as part of the entry, enabling real-time tracking of your position, or you can rent your own for specific events and this will allow friends and family to follow your progress. The apps Strava Beacon and FollowMee give a very basic map which is not of value for navigation. Phone-based apps will require mobile phone signals. GSM or LTE trackers have a SIM card that operates on all networks, but some kind of mobile

OS Locate, an app for your phone from Ordnance Survey, will give you your full grid reference and also includes a compass, so you can see in which direction you are heading.

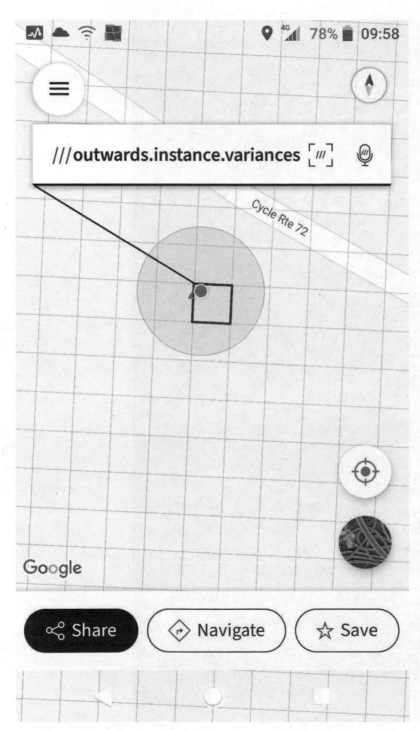

///outwards.instance.variances

Cycle Rte 72

Google

⇄ Share   ◈ Navigate   ☆ Save

What3Words will give you a three-word code for your location. Mountain Rescue advise that this can sometimes be inaccurate in remote places and that nearby squares may have similar sounding words. This will be important when giving the code over the phone.

'If you are completely lost, admit it and call for help'

phone signal is required so these won't work in remote areas.

For races in remote areas, it is worth considering buying or renting a satellite tracker. Two types are available: SPOT trackers and Iridium trackers. Both have pros and cons, so check which suits your needs best.

The weather can have a major impact on navigation. If mist or fog develops you will not be able to see key navigation markers. If you are on high ground, aim to descend. Preferably retrace your steps: your GPS watch may help. Your route will of course look completely different going the other way. Aim to take well-trodden paths heading down and beware of following sheep tracks. Ideally try to use your map. Take great care if out in the mountains in fog that you do not walk/run to dangerous descents. If you are completely lost, admit it and call for help.

If you are unhurt and mountain rescue can pinpoint where you are and there is a good mobile signal, they may be able to talk you down off the mountain.

First aid

There is no absolute requirement for first-aid training if you are going out running, but it does make sense to undertake some basic training. Minor injuries are common on trail events and being able to offer a fellow runner assistance is highly desirable. There are many organisations offering training but it is worth seeking out specific training relevant to your needs. Courses are not expensive and can usually be done as a group. I have listed several useful books on outdoor first aid in the Further Reading section, but they are not a substitute for hands-on practical training.

Other than a small first-aid kit, useful lightweight items that can be carried on longer off-road runs are foil blankets (the body cools rapidly when you stop running) and a triangular bandage which can be used for all manner of dressings and slings. Cohesive tape that sticks to itself is extremely valuable for holding dressings in place.

Insurance

Insurance is certainly something to consider seriously. It is worth considering sport-specific insurance, which should cover cash benefits for injury and temporary disablement, private health contributions as well as personal liability. Policies will usually cover legal expenses and search and rescue fees, the cost depending on the type of sport undertaken and the geographical limits. Sportscover Direct provide good-value policies. While you may think this unnecessary, accidents can occur at any time and can have a significant impact, for example on your ability to work. Having travel insurance if travelling abroad is essential. It is important to check that the travel insurance covers participation in sporting events.

5 | BASICS OF TRAINING

Sample training programmes are widely available online, in monthly running magazines and any number of books (*see* Resources). However just as everyone's feet are different, everyone's training needs are different and off-the-peg training programmes may not necessarily suit every runner. If you are following a training programme and it is not working for you, consider trying a different one or getting in touch with a running coach who can develop a bespoke programme based on your level of fitness and goals. One size definitely does not fit all.

Even if you have no plans for anything other than social running, it still makes sense to incorporate some non-running training, so that you enjoy your running more. Afterall, if the aim is to be able to chat with your friends while running you need to do some training to ensure that you are not just huffing and puffing after them.

I shall cover the various general principles regarding training to help you make the best choices in terms of a routine. For me, the most important factor is making sure that training remains enjoyable as well as preparing me for whichever events I intend to enter. While I like to have an overall routine, I also like to mix up my training so I don't get bored. This chapter covers the basics of running biology, running style and economy and the ways of monitoring training.

There are some key principles to training which I have learnt over the years:

1. To be good at running you need to run
This is self-evident, but you need to consider what your running goals are and adjust your running accordingly. You will need to plan your training to improve your running, so that you gradually increase the effort over time but in a

---

GOOD HABITS

Train in a structured way to develop good habits – don't try to wing it on race day:

- Training will help you avoid injury (training to train: this is sometimes referred to as pre-conditioning)
- Training will improve your form and fitness
- Training allows you to develop and understand what works best for you, including practising race-day strategies
- A good, varied training programme will help you stay motivated

structured way. It is helpful to do other types of exercise if you are not an elite runner, but there are no shortcuts.

2. Quality not quantity is the key

People mistake volume of miles for effective training. You can run for miles with no appreciable improvement in fitness: junk miles. Each run needs to have a purpose: slow recovery run, interval training (long medium-paced intervals, short fast intervals), hill reps, tempo run (just less than best race pace), trail run and so on. To run a marathon, you do not need to be training over huge distances all the time. If you have never run a marathon before and have signed up for one more in hope than expectation, then be reassured that training distances up to half-marathon will be more than adequate to get you round, although it is good to have one long, slow practice run of about 20 miles six weeks before, just to get the feel of what a really long run is like and work out how to drink and eat enough to last you through to the finish while avoiding hitting the dreaded 'wall'.

For older runners, the amount of time for recovery is longer, and less training is probably better.

You may want to use some races as part of your training programme, as you will be encouraged to run harder in a race environment than you might out on your own or with your training partners. Races can give you a benchmark of how you are progressing. If the target is a major distance, then races over shorter distances will be helpful. The races also give you the opportunity to practise feeding and hydration strategies and refine pre-race and post-race strategies before the really big day.

3. Choose the best time to train

New studies have suggested that for optimal benefit from training, men and women may need to train at different times of day. This is linked to the circadian rhythm and its effect on hormone levels. Women seeking to reduce

> *'The best time in the day to train varies according to age, sex and fitness goals'*

body fat and blood pressure will get most benefit from training in the morning. However, for women trying to improve muscle strength and mood, it is better to exercise in the evening. For men wanting to improve mood, metabolic health and reduce risks of diabetes, obesity and heart disease, then exercising in the evening is more effective than the morning.

4. Adequate rest is vital

You need to ensure that you have adequate rest between training episodes. Overtraining is very easy and there are few warning signs until it is too late. The more expensive sports watches now incorporate software that analyses your training and identifies when you are pushing too hard, and when your training is unproductive. Rest means rest. It does not mean going off for a long, hard cycle with friends. Rest also does not mean being completely inactive, so a reasonable walk is OK. A basic guide is one day of active rest per week, one weekend off per month and one month with a marked reduction in activity per year. I tend to find that the period in the run-up to Christmas is always busy with other things, so use this to cut back on training. Then of course, come the New Year, one is refreshed and ready to get going again to work off all the mince pies.

Monitoring your resting heart rate can be valuable: a rising resting heart rate is often an early warning sign of inadequate rest and/or overtraining. Take it seriously.

> ## *'Make sure you get enough rest and sleep'*

Equally getting enough good-quality sleep is important (*see* 'Sleep Hygiene', Chapter 4).

5. Strength and HIIT training is valuable

Strength and conditioning training is valuable to improve performance and HIIT (high intensity interval training) is excellent for improving fitness. Including these into the training routine is really important, and this reduces the tendency to just add another run of junk miles (*see* Chapter 6).

6. Listen to your body

While it might seem obvious, listening to what your body is telling you is crucial. Be prepared to have a break and rest if you are tired. We all have days when we really don't feel like pulling on the trainers and going for a run, and while it is important to maintain the mental discipline of training, it may be wise to accept that shortening the run, doing something different or doing nothing may be wise.

7. Get used to the mental discipline of training

Most of running is actually about the mental aspects. The science tells us that your brain will start saying it is tired as a way of protecting your muscles, long before the muscles are exhausted. There is a need therefore to maintain a mental discipline and not just stop at the first signs of tiredness, while listening to your body as above. Routine is valuable. Running with friends makes getting out easier: you are less likely to skip the training run. The caution is that you may feel pressured to run when you really shouldn't, or you run faster than is appropriate. Be prepared to be firm with yourself and your friends.

8. Training is not all about 'no pain, no gain'

It is a fallacy to say that to benefit from training there should be pain. There is a difference between pushing hard and causing pain (usually an indicator of injury or overtraining). Finding the right balance is important. Pushing yourself in training until you collapse is not helpful. Training is about incremental increases in the training stress applied over time, which pushes the body to adapt without pushing it to a state of exhaustion. If you are training in a group, you need to look at yourself, not unthinkingly try to keep up with the superfit hares. Your 'hard' may be someone else's 'easy', but that doesn't matter, it is still hard for you. Injury is more likely to come from pushing yourself to keep up with those who are fitter/faster. Ideally train with people of similar ability and goals.

9. Keep a training log

It is worthwhile keeping a training log. This is useful as part of periodisation of your training (*see* Chapter 6) and for being able to see how far you have come (literally and figuratively). It is also worth recording your times for any races you do and keeping a record of your personal bests (PBs). Runners live and die by their PBs, but try to avoid becoming obsessed by them. A race/run is not a failure because you didn't beat your PB, as long as you enjoyed it.

> ## *'A race/run is not a failure because you didn't beat your PB, as long as you enjoyed it'*

If the race did not go to plan, you have your training record, you can review it and see whether a poor race can be explained by problems with your training or other factors. You can download Excel templates for recording training, make your own (*see* Resources) or just use a notebook. The downside of all the logs is being able to see the reduction in speed with age, although I console myself that I can now run further than I ever did when I was younger.

10. Be careful how quickly you build up your mileage

As you get fitter there is often a compulsion to push yourself to run further each week. The more rapidly you increase your mileage and the greater the increase, the greater your chances of injury. If you have done the basic training and are fit, you can increase your mileage by up to 30 per cent in a week. You can also escalate your mileage more quickly if you are fit but have had a short lay-off. It is very important to have proper down times when you reduce your training to allow recovery and repair – this is the concept of periodisation of training.

11. Be careful about sharing your activities on social media and fitness sites

There can be great benefits to sharing your achievements via social media and this can be positive for other readers. Having a virtual running community to interact with can be helpful and increase motivation and provide support if you are finding the training tough. However, it can have a negative effect on some people, with stress from the pressure to perform, post something, compete with others, run/train harder than you should and this can lead to unhealthy obsessive/compulsive and addictive behaviours. This has been described as 'compare and despair'. Be prepared to do runs with no gadgets and set limits on your social media interactions. At the end of the day, only you matter.

KEY FEATURES OF GOOD TRAINING

- Plan your training
- Incorporate both running and non-running training (HIIT, cycling, swimming)
- Incorporate strength training
- Vary the type of running (short and fast, long and slow, intervals)
- Quality over quantity – avoid junk miles
- Learn about periodisation
- Train yourself mentally to cope with the discomfort of running
- Make sure you have adequate rest and sleep
- Choose the best time to train
- Keep a log and monitor your training
- Build up your training gradually, especially running mileage
- Listen to your body and be prepared to adapt your training
- Keep a check on resting heart rate
- Look at your diet and make sure you are getting enough calories for the level of activity

12. Three key basic elements

Mara Yamauchi, one of the UK's top female marathon runners, distils the basics of running into three elements: training, fuel and rest (*see* Further Reading). All are equally important. She stresses the need to keep things simple and not to over-complicate or over-think your running. Never lose sight of these elements – all are important, especially the rest!

MUSCLE AND TENDONS

Clearly the key components of the body that are required to run are the muscles and tendons, together with the nervous system to provide co-ordination and control. The science of muscles, tendons and nerves is complex, but the following are some basic facts.

1. There are different types of muscle fibres

- **Type I: slow twitch fibres.** These are the fibres required for endurance running as they are relatively resistant to fatigue. They are designed mainly for aerobic activity (oxygen requiring) and have a high capacity for fat burning. They do not increase dramatically in size with training.
- **Type II: fast twitch fibres.** Fast twitch fibres are really designed for anaerobic metabolism (without oxygen), burning glucose to produce lactate. However, with training, Type IIa fibres can become effective at aerobic metabolism as well. Type II fibres increase in size when subjected to strength training. To be a good sprinter you need to have mainly fast twitch fibres.

While there is a genetic element to the number and type of muscle fibres an individual has, training can adjust the percentages. A sprinter will have only 15 per cent slow twitch fibres, while a marathon runner will have 80 per cent. Women tend to have more slow twitch fibres than men, which explains why women perform as well as or better than men over the longest distances.

2. Tendons are like springs

Tendons, which join muscles to bones, behave like springs in that they have a degree of elasticity. It takes force to stretch them and then the force can be released to create movement (elastic recoil). Jump-based exercises are particularly good for improving tendons' elastic recoil but like all body tissues, overuse can cause damage. The Achilles tendon is the major tendon involved in running, and calf raise exercises to condition it are wise. People with hypermobility have lax tendons, and will therefore get less elastic recoil. Minor degrees of hypermobility are common and are not a bar to running. However more significant hypermobility can be a problem, so specific advice from a sports physiotherapist may be wise.

Tendons have little in the way of blood supply, so injuries to tendons always take much longer to heal than injuries to the muscles to which they are attached; it is as well to treat them with respect. Extreme stress can cause rupture of tendons and where the Achilles tendon is involved, that means a long period in a cast or even surgery to repair it.

3. Both muscles and tendons have specialised sensory nerves

The commands to muscles to contract come from the nervous system and ultimately from the brain. However, a lot of the actual integrated movement is mediated by local reflexes. Muscles and tendons have specialised sensory organs which measure the activity and stretch and this information is used to control contraction. These sensory elements (muscle spindles) provide sensory information that is used to control balance.

4. Muscles need a good blood supply

Muscles require a large volume of blood. The incoming blood delivers oxygen, glucose, fats, and amino acids for muscle building and repair. Outgoing blood is taken away in the venules and veins, removing carbon dioxide, lactate and other elements produced by muscle use and damage. One of the effects of training is to increase the network of capillaries by creating new ones (capillarisation), especially as muscles increase in size, thus improving the delivery of oxygen and nutrients to the muscles and enabling them to work more efficiently.

5. Muscles need a continuous supply of nutrients

Muscles store some glycogen and have a tick-over of the manufacture of the main immediate energy compounds. The stores of immediately available energy are enough to power the muscles for a few seconds only (think of sprint races) and after that energy comes from breakdown of the glycogen in the muscle and liver to produce glucose. This will last for about

> *'The more you train, the better your muscles become at fat burning'*

90 minutes of running before it is exhausted, assuming that the stores were at maximum capacity and depending on the intensity of exercise. After this, muscles have to burn fats, which will be released into the circulation from fat stores. Part of the purpose of training is to make the muscles better at burning fat and less reliant on stores of glycogen.

The more you train, the better your muscles become at fat burning.

AEROBIC AND ANAEROBIC METABOLISM

Muscle metabolism is complex but the two most important aspects to remember are aerobic and anaerobic metabolism.

- *Aerobic metabolism* is where the muscles are using a mixture of fat and glucose, with oxygen. This gives the maximal amount of energy to the muscles and is suitable for longer runs.
- *Anaerobic metabolism* is where glucose predominantly is burnt without oxygen to form lactate and energy. This reaction in the muscles does not require oxygen, but is only suitable for short bursts of high intensity activity such as sprints, as lactate accumulates briefly in the blood stream and muscles (lactic acid burn). Training improves the capacity of the muscles to handle lactic acid and to switch muscles to burning more fat than glucose.

Everyone, no matter what your preferred running distance, benefits from some anaerobic (speed) work. This will enable you to put in that final kick in the last kilometre and sprint for the line. This means doing fast interval training, with the duration and speed of the intervals varied according to your racing targets.

WHO TAUGHT YOU TO RUN?

The majority of people have never been 'taught' to run. As you will see at any mass participation event, running styles are as varied as the people present. If your goal is to get from A to B and have fun, then running style doesn't really matter, as long as you do not suffer any injuries. However, a lot of academic and commercial research goes into studying how people run and trying to work out which running style is most effective. Shoe manufacturers in particularly are very interested in how shoe design may assist. This led Nike to their controversial race shoes with carbon fibre plates, which propelled Eliud Kipchoge to a (paced) sub-two-hour marathon.

Advancing knowledge has led to re-evaluation of running styles, and you can buy any number of books advising you on how to change your running style to improve your performance and prevent injury. I have read my way through a few of these, which are often written with messianic fervour, and many are completely impenetrable. While they are interesting, it is difficult to apply the written information without involving a coach.

Do you need to change your running style? The answer for most of us is no! Everyone's body is a different shape, and on the whole there is not a lot you can do about it. So, if you are pigeon toed or have duck feet, that isn't going to be amenable to retraining. The good news is that neither of these styles have any impact on average performance.

Broadly speaking, people are divided into fore-foot strikers and heel strikers, defined by which bit of the foot hits the ground first. Again, it doesn't seem to matter which you are and trying to change you from one to the other can be difficult and may cause more problems than it solves. You can tell which you are by looking at the wear on the soles of your trainers. The photographs demonstrate a good running style throughout the gait cycle. Note the powerful push off.

An example of a good running style through the complete gait cycle.

An example of a worn-out trainer. The outsole at the point of heel-strike has worn through to the soft foam underneath, which is being rapidly destroyed. Time to change to a new pair!

The key to understanding when help is required is injury, particularly repeated injury. This is usually the main pointer to there being something wrong with the running style or with the running shoes. Shoes are discussed in Chapter 3, but suffice it to say that many injuries are as a result of worn-out or inappropriate shoes.

Another issue that affects running style and economy is structural imbalance. We naturally tend to have a stronger and weaker side. The body is not symmetrical: the heart is on the left, the liver on the right. There may be imbalances of muscle groups (typically the quads at the front of the thigh are stronger than the hamstrings at the back). The imbalances may contribute to an increased susceptibility to injuries or impact on performance. Wear patterns on the soles of your shoes may give a clue if they are different for each foot. Getting a friend or coach to video you running from head on, side and behind will be very revealing.

Below are some key rules that I have distilled from the information available and from personal experience.

1. Your running style

Your running style is largely going to be defined by your anatomy, what shape you are, which is in turn defined by your genetic make-up. However, it can be tweaked.

2. The most common running style problem

The most common running style problem is overstriding, that is taking steps that are too long. Taking shorter steps at a faster rate and having a little more heel lift is better. Learning how to do this can be difficult.

3. Repeated injuries/pain suggest a problem that needs to be investigated

If your running is hampered by repeated injuries, particularly in the same area, then you need to start thinking about causes. These can be related to shoes, to running style and volume and type of training. If the shoes aren't the problem, then next consider running style.

4. Changing running style needs external help

If you think there is a problem with your running style, get professional advice from a running coach who understands gait analysis. Gait analysis should involve side-on, front-on and rear-on video recording. Changing the style of running will undoubtedly require a course of remedial exercises. Finding a reasonable expert can be a bit of a lottery, and word of mouth tends to be best. Running club members may be able to advise.

5. Poor running style can be linked to weak and imbalanced muscles

A lot of running gait and injury problems can be linked to weak or imbalanced muscles in the legs, around the hips and in the lower back, particularly the gluteal muscles. Doing exercises that strengthen these muscles can significantly improve running performance and style.

6. Rigid orthotic inserts into running shoes are unlikely to help

Some people with running-related problems are advised to get rigid thermoplastic inserts for running shoes, supposedly to 'correct' the anatomical abnormalities that cause the injuries. Most of the evidence suggests that this approach is usually unhelpful and may actually make the problem worse or create new problems. However, you can replace a worn insole with a new soft spongy insole. Most shoes are sold with thin flimsy insoles (to reduce weight), and it can be useful to change to a more cushioned version.

7. Get advice on selecting shoes

The key here is that shoes must be the right size and must be instantly comfortable in the shop. Do not be afraid to try lots of pairs. Buying shoes that you have never used before over the internet is risky (unless you can return them easily).

8. Don't obsess over running style unless you have a problem

Unless you have injuries or are the next Olympic hopeful, obsessing over your running style is unnecessary – just run and enjoy yourself. Evidence suggests that running regularly naturally improves your running style and efficiency. However, if you have repeated or persistent injuries then it is worth seeing a coach capable of analysing your running style and

> *'Unless you have injuries or are the next Olympic hopeful, obsessing over your running style is unnecessary – just run and enjoy yourself'*

suggesting improvements and exercises that will help.

9. Training properly is important

Doing the right sort of training and having plenty of rest days is very important. If you run when you are too tired, your running style will deteriorate and increase the likelihood of injuries. Concentrate on maintaining a good posture and don't just shuffle along. Remember, with training, less can be more and it is quality not quantity that matters. Varying the training through intervals, hill reps, running downhill (harder than you think) and varying the pace of runs is crucial. Every training run should have a goal.

RUNNING ECONOMY

The most successful runners tend to be those with the best running economy. Simply put, your running economy is how much oxygen you need to progress at a given pace. If you are not running in an economical manner, then the oxygen demand will go up and this will increase the work related to breathing. Running economy is a complex issue but there are key factors which may be amenable to improvement.

1. Running style

The three most important biomechanical factors in your running style which contribute to running economy are the degree of vertical oscillation (how much your body bounces up and down), the step length and frequency, and how efficient your footstrike is. The aim is to have a running style with shorter, faster steps which will mean less vertical oscillation. To help with the efficiency of your footstrike, choose your shoes wisely and do not run in worn-out shoes, which will have a significant negative effect on running efficiency.

2. Metabolism

The type of fuel that your muscles are burning will have a significant impact on your running economy and one of the key features of training is to improve your muscles' ability to burn fat rather than glucose or glycogen. This applies particularly to endurance events (see 'Nutrition', Chapter 4). Your overall weight and fat and glycogen reserves have an impact on your running economy.

3. Environmental aspects

Running in extremes of heat and cold has an additional metabolic cost to the body in terms of maintaining the correct core temperature. Energy spent in these activities therefore is not available to the muscles for running. Select clothing that is appropriate to the environmental conditions and take steps to minimise the impact, such as running in the coolest parts of the day.

4. Genetic factors

Finally, there are genetic factors which will have a significant impact on running economy. These include your anatomical features and muscle structure, by which we mean the balance of fast and slow twitch muscle fibres.

There is not a great deal you can do about the genetic factors.

WARM UP AND COOL DOWN

Some coaches recommend pre-conditioning, which is training to train (see Shepherd, *Strength Training for Runners* in Further Reading). The concept here is that to train effectively, you need to get the muscles and cardiovascular system into a fit state to work. This involves a series of exercises, designed to address common areas of weakness and reduce the risks of injury. In particular, these address the importance of improving tendon elasticity. Exercises should work on the Achilles tendon, hamstrings (prone to injury), the gluteal muscles and the quads. The hardest that muscles will work is when they lengthen. This typically affects the quads when running downhill and calf muscles: squats and lunges are useful exercises.

One of the areas of the body that gets ignored in training are the feet. The feet are made up of lots of tendons and muscles and these play a very important role in gait and running. As you get into running these muscles will enlarge to cope with the extra workload, which is why as you run more you will find that your feet increase in size (usually by half a size at least). Exercises for the small muscles in the feet will help prepare your feet for more efficient running. Bateman and Jones (*Older yet Faster* – see Further Reading) have a whole chapter devoted to exercises for the feet. At least consider doing a basic claw exercise with the toes: dig the toes into a carpet and pull each foot forward in turn.

If you are just starting out on your running career, it makes sense to get into the habit of doing some basic pre-conditioning exercises as well as just trying to run, as your muscles will be unfamiliar with the demands you are trying to place on them. All the evidence suggests that the best exercises for warm-up are dynamic, that is involving movement, rather than static stretches. Good basic exercises (use YouTube or the *Runners' World* website to identify good technique) are:

1. Calf stretches: Stand with the balls of the feet on a step, lower your heels below the level of the step and then push back up so the heel is above the step and repeat. You can start with both feet on the step, then move to just having one foot on the step at a time.
2. Squats: Do these on both feet and progress to single-leg squats. Ensure as you squat that you look forward and try to keep the back as upright as possible.
3. Do forward bends at the hips to touch your toes, keeping the back straight (by looking forward as you bend).
4. Lunges: Step forward with one leg and keeping the shin of the leading leg vertical, lower the knee of the trailing leg to the ground (or as close as you can get it). Keep your back vertical. Then bring back the leading leg, stand upright and repeat with the opposite leg. Alternatively, this can be done as a progressive lunge walk.
5. Jogging on the spot is a good warm-up. You can modify this to include high knees (lift each leg in turn so the thigh is parallel with the ground) and heel kicks (flick your heel up behind you). Doing side steps (+/- arm swings) is also helpful and loosens the muscles on the inside of the thigh.
6. Warm up the arms with arms swings (doing standing breaststroke and front/back crawl movements are excellent) and do body twists to loosen up the trunk muscles.

Muscles are not just motors that pull on the tendons to create movement. There is a complex sensory system built into the muscles and tendons, and the feedback is transmitted to the brain for overall integration. Part of the role of the sensory element in muscles and tendons is concerned with balance. Training up the neuromuscular co-ordination therefore is an important part of preparing for running, for example by doing drills requiring you to exercise on one leg or carrying out exercises on a wobble board or Bosu ball. Having good balance is important for running economy on roads but becomes much more important when running off-road. Equally, running off-road is excellent for improving balance and co-ordination.

There is debate about how much of a warm-up is required before running. Overall, an active dynamic warm-up is probably most valuable. The purpose of this is to warm up the muscles through a series of active exercises. This in turn increases the blood flow to the muscles and gets the breathing and circulation ready for exercise. The warm-up also gets you mentally into the best state to perform. A good warm-up should be five to ten minutes, but obviously not at a level that exhausts the body before you start your run or exercise programme. For older runners a good warm-up is even more important, as older muscles take longer to get going.

Some coaches simply recommend a slow warm-up run at an easy pace for ten minutes before the start of, say, an interval session or threshold run. If you are about to do a marathon or beyond then the first mile or so is your warm-up – take it slowly.

'For older runners a good warm-up is even more important, as older muscles take longer to get going'

After a run there is some evidence to suggest that static stretching may help. However, if you have been doing a hard anaerobic session such as sprint intervals, working the muscle hard and producing a lot of lactate, then a ten-minute cool down run at an easy pace to keep the circulation moving vigorously will ensure that the lactate produced is returned to the liver. If there are any niggles at the end of the run then targeted stretches, foam rolling, using a spiky ball or percussion massager may all be helpful. Yoga stretches are an excellent way of dealing with tight muscles from training.

A WORD ON BREATHING

Breathing is something we take for granted. It is one of the bodily functions that the brain controls automatically without the need for conscious effort. We can of course override it. Breathing properly is important for getting oxygen into the blood and getting rid of carbon dioxide. When running, if breathing gets too fast the exchange of gases is impaired. Sometimes it is important to take control, slow the rate of breathing and increase the depth of each breath rather than just panting. Another useful technique, used in patients with damaged lungs, is to breathe out through pursed lips. This increases the dwell time of the air in the alveoli, which do not collapse, and increases the time for gas exchange. Over-breathing (hyperventilation) can cause a problem if too much carbon dioxide is lost, as this makes the blood more alkali. This causes tingling in the extremities and cramps in the muscles, as well as feelings of dizziness and possibly fainting.

Breathing through the nose is also important, rather than just panting with an open mouth. The nose has a number of key functions, all of which help running. Obviously, the passages are narrower than the mouth, so if there is a need to get a lot of air in quickly the mouth is better.

RATE OF PERCEIVED EXERTION

The rate of perceived exertion (RPE) is a well-established subjective scale for monitoring and setting the intensity of exercise. It enables you to work out your lactate threshold. This is important for determining the level at which you train: so-called tempo (threshold) runs should be at just below your lactate threshold – a fast pace but one where the rate of lactate production from the muscles is balanced by the body's ability to remove lactate to the liver to be recycled into glucose. This equates to an RPE of between four and five. While the RPE scale is subjective, for an individual it is useful, and if you are not sure how hard you should be training then it provides a good guide. It is worth, in the beginning at least, recording the RPE of training sessions in your training log. After a while you'll become tuned into your body and will know what the effective RPE for a given activity is. You need to ensure that your training contains sessions at different levels on the RPE scale, although obviously you will only be using levels 7–10 sparingly and for short periods of time/distance. Remember that it is essential to do a proper warm-up before starting any seriously hard exercise or you will risk injury.

RPE Scale
  0 = No effort
  1 = Very, very easy (walking)
  2 = Very easy
  3 = Moderate (half marathon/marathon pace)
  4 = Somewhat hard (lactate threshold pace, 10k training pace)
  5 = Hard
  6 = Harder (5k pace)
  7 = Very hard
  8 = Very, very hard
  9 = Extremely hard
  10 = Maximal effort (all-out sprint for the line at the end of a race)

USE OF HEART RATE MONITORS

The use of heart rate monitoring is now more widespread, as more and more sports watches have the facility. This can either be measured at the wrist or by a linked chest monitor. It is however very easy to become obsessed with the technical data produced by the current generation of mid- to high-end watches, so it is good discipline sometimes to just go for a run, enjoy it and avoid looking at the watch until the end.

The aim of using the HRM is to tailor your training and to monitor intensity. The HRM will also give you an indication of over-training (raised resting heart rate).

If you wear your sports watch with HRM all the time, you will get a measurement of your baseline resting heart rate. As you get fitter this will slowly decline; 50–60 will be usual, but super-elite athletes may get their resting heart rate down to 38–40. A rising resting heart rate, assuming you are not ill, is a marker of overtraining. If you have heart rhythm problems the watches may give unusual readings. If you are known to have a heart rhythm problem, then you should check with your doctor before exercising. If you find very high resting heart rates, you should also consult your doctor.

For training purposes, heart rate is divided into zones. These are calculated as a percentage of your maximum heart rate (MHR), which is calculated in relation to your age. The old formula for calculating MHR was simply 220 - age. However, this has been revised to 208 -(0.7 × age). Once you have this you can calculate your own zones:

Zone 1: very light 50–60% MHR
Zone 2: light 60–70% MHR
Zone 3: moderate 70–80% MHR
Zone 4: hard 80–90% MHR
Zone 5: very hard 90–100% MHR

Most watches will automatically calculate your MHR once you enter your age on set up and will therefore calculate the training zones appropriate for you (and record the data of how much time you have spent in each zone during a workout). This relieves you of the chore of doing the maths yourself. A simpler system is to use the American College of Sports Medicine guidance:

Aerobic training	50–70% MHR
Tempo and threshold	71–85% MHR
Intervals	>85% MHR

Sometimes the heart rate reserve (HRR) is used. This is calculated by subtracting the measured resting heart rate from the calculated maximum heart rate (or 220 - age). This gives the working range of the heart rate and can also be used to calculate the training zones on an individualised basis. This is the Karvonen formula and on-line calculators are available (*see* Resources). You can also calculate your target heart rate for particular exercise sessions and use the HRM to check that you are achieving it. You may need to alter the default screens on your watch to ensure that the heart rate is highly visible.

Most benefit from training will come from work in Zones 3–5, and you need to have a training programme that includes work in all three zones for maximal benefit.

VO$_2$ MAX AND POWER

You will see VO$_2$ max referred to extensively in relation to exercise and it is a major currency of the level of fitness. VO$_2$ max is a measure of the body's ability to take up and utilise oxygen. Obviously the higher the figure the better your body is at utilising oxygen. However, the correlation between the figures for VO$_2$ max and actual performance is poor. VO$_2$ max is a measure of cardiorespiratory fitness, but athletic performance also depends on other factors. Accurate measures of VO$_2$ max require testing in physiological laboratories, but many of the high-end sports watches are able to estimate VO_2 max, based on running heart rate and pace over a minimum of ten minutes. It can also be estimated from resting heart rate, age and activity, and by incorporating heart rate variability.

All of these measures are estimates. When various watches were compared against laboratory-based measurements (as the gold standard), most watches overestimated the VO_2 max. The results were worse when wrist-based HRM was used and worse in men than women (unexplained). Overall, the results from watches appear to be accurate to within 5 per cent and are probably reasonably consistent for a given watch on the same person. This means that the figures are not useless and over time may be helpful. However, comparing your VO_2 max to a friend who is using a different watch is not going to be meaningful.

The Cooper test is a simple test that you can do for yourself to calculate your VO_2 max. You need to choose a flat level surface to run on and then you record how far you run in twelve minutes (an athletics track is ideal). Your VO_2 max is (22.35 × distance in kilometres) - 11.29 or (35.96 × distance in miles) - 11.29.

Measurement of power has been used to measure fitness for cyclists for a long time. It is a new concept for runners, mainly because it is much harder to measure. At the moment, there are no defined figures for good and bad, so the role of power for runners is as a comparative figure to demonstrate training progression. It will enable you to monitor power output throughout a race. There are several devices coming onto the market that will enable runners to measure power; each has its own idiosyncrasies.

Does any of this matter to average runners? The answer to this is almost certainly no. While it is interesting to see, once you know what your VO_2 max and power are, it is unlikely to change much on a day-to-day basis, although looking for a trend to improvement over months might be realistic. For high-performance athletes, VO_2 max and power are more important, as parameters of training progress and fitness.

6 | TYPES OF TRAINING

You will probably be reading this book because you want to run or are already running. You will have goals for your running, even if they are very simple: get fit, keep fit, lose weight. Goals change over time, and once you are hooked on running you may start seeking new and different run-related challenges. While I am not a fan of New Year's resolutions (remember gyms make most of their profit in the first three months of the year) it is a good time to evaluate what your goals for the year will be. Training cannot and should not be at the same level all the time and needs to be adjusted up and down according to goals. Often you will have your eye on a particular personal goal: do a parkrun, run a fast 5k or 10k, run your first half-marathon/marathon/ultra for example. Each target needs to have a specific programme, so that whatever event you have chosen, you can perform the best you can and, more importantly, enjoy the event and avoid injury.

Even if you have no specific race or event in mind, it is still worth considering planning your training in a structured way, so that you get more out of it and are less likely to get bored and give up.

Planning ahead is sensible, to give your body enough time to adapt to the training load. For almost any event you plan to enter, specific training programmes can be found online or in running magazines, including those starting from scratch. However, these programmes

> *'Each target needs to have a specific training programme, so that whatever event you have chosen, you can perform the best you can and, more importantly, enjoy the event and avoid injury'*

are not interactive, they don't tell you how to cope when things aren't going according to plan. This is why joining a running club can be so useful; there are real people who have the experience on how to advise both informally (other runners) and formally through their qualified coaches. Online or distance coaching is available. You can monitor progress in a training log.

The key to training is to ensure that every activity has a purpose in your training plan. It is very easy to just get into the habit of running junk miles; jogging gently for 6 miles may give you less fitness improvement than a harder run for 3 miles. There is still a place for the longer easy recovery run but it has the specific purpose of allowing recovery.

Improving fitness requires that you gradually increase load, so that the body adapts. The adaptive response to an increase in training load is quite slow, about 21–28 days, so do not expect an instant improvement and equally do not try to ramp up the training too quickly. The increase in load can be in either volume or intensity or both. Volume can increase either in the length of individual runs or the total weekly volume. Intensity will be based around the pace and what you do in the runs. This has been studied since the 1940s and is referred to as the General Adaptation Syndrome (GAS), formulated by Hans Selye. His theory defines three effects of training on the body:

- An initial 'alarm phase' when a training stimulus greater than usual is imposed
- A 'resistance phase' as the body adapts to the extra stimulus and is able to cope/resist it
- An 'exhaustion phase' when continued exposure to the increasing training leads to exhaustion and deterioration in capability

To monitor intensity at the most basic level will require a sports watch which will give you distance, time and pace. Training needs to address both speed (= intensity: shorter, faster runs) and endurance (=volume: longer, slower runs). Building endurance is essential for races over 5k: it involves training the muscles to burn fat rather than rely on glucose and its precursor glycogen, and improving cardiovascular fitness.

Short speed-work intervals are essentially anaerobic (meaning that the muscle is using stored resources and isn't dependent on oxygen). Doing explosive strength training and plyometrics (jump-based training) is excellent for speed but if you want to run long distances, endurance is best developed by low-intensity, high-volume training. Everyone, no matter what their distance goals are, should do some speed work.

Think about varying the nature of the run and mix up different types. Vary distances and speeds, incorporate running uphill and downhill, intervals, use trails and roads. Watch your total mileage. Without being ageist, older runners should be aiming for lower mileages and more rest days, as recovery is slower. Decide before you go out what type of run you

ACTIVITIES TO INCORPORATE INTO A GOOD TRAINING PROGRAMME

- Vary distance (short, medium and long) and pace of each session (base, threshold, VO$_2$ max)
- Use intervals
- Use hill sprints
- Practise running downhill
- Go off-road to improve balance and reduce impact on joints
- Practise walk-run if you are planning long races
- Use back-to-back runs (running on consecutive days, vary pace/distance)
- Two runs in a day (vary pace/distance)
- Strength and conditioning sessions, HIIT, circuit training
- Cross-training
- Race specific training (night running, running in heat/cold, navigation)

will do but be flexible: if your planned activity isn't going well, change it or stop – there is always another day.

How fast should I be running?

You should have sessions at different paces. The pace and duration of runs will depend on your goals and your level of fitness. Sprint sessions at VO_2 max are necessary to improve speed – these are maximal efforts and will usually be as sprint intervals. Threshold runs are longer; working at just below the lactate threshold is valuable for improving fitness and the ability of muscles to burn fat. At threshold you should find talking difficult! Your base runs will be slower than threshold. The aim of the base run is as either recovery runs after more intense sessions or to build up tolerance to running for longer distances and/or for longer. You will also see the term 'tempo run': this can mean either a threshold run, a longer run at just below the lactate threshold or a shorter run at above the lactate threshold (*see* page 79).

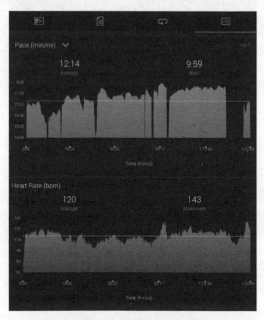

Stats from a typical tempo run.

You can use the different paces in your regular runs, for example by including a period of threshold running into an easy run or doing fast surges.

The pace at which you should run depends on your level of fitness and overall goals: you can use your watch to measure your pace on different-length runs and compare this with your heart rate and RPE. You will soon learn to gauge your running times.

A lot is made of the 80/20 rule, where only 20 per cent of your training should be hard and the rest easy to moderate. This is a useful rule if you are planning to run long distances (half-marathon and above) and are doing a lot of miles in training, but it may not work so well for those training for shorter distances and/or doing a limited weekly mileage.

How far should I be running?

This depends on your level of fitness and your running goals. It's the quality that matters, not the distance. If you are planning to enter a half-marathon, you need a long, slow run up to 8–10 miles every few weeks and probably need to do a test run of close to the target distance a couple of months before. This test should not be so close to the event that you are still recovering by the time the event comes round. If you have never run a half-marathon, then it is good to know that you can manage the distance. You will be able to practise fuelling, hydration and learn how best to cope with the time on your feet. Likewise for a marathon, you need to have training runs in the range

'It's the quality that matters, not the distance'

of 10–15 miles and perhaps a slightly longer test run several months before. The rest of the training should be over shorter distances and at faster pace (5–10k or 3–6 miles)

Intervals

Intervals are valuable as a way of increasing the training load. Like other aspects of training, it is important to define the purpose of the interval training, for example working on a faster finish, being able to sustain a faster pace for longer. Interval training should wait until you have achieved a basic level of running fitness. Always warm up properly before starting intervals with at least ten minutes easy running and do a similar length cool-down after the interval set. Older runners take longer to warm up, so this should be borne in mind. No more than two interval sessions should be done per week, and each session should have a planned recovery session after. Interval training can be applied to any form of exercise, not just running, although what follows is specifically about running.

Interval training can be 'bottom up' where a target pace is identified and the distance is gradually increased, or 'top down' where the distance is fixed but the pace is gradually increased over time. The distance or speed should be appropriate to your goals. So, if you are planning to improve your 5k time, then the distance of the interval will be shorter than if you are planning to run a marathon (yes, marathon runners should still be doing intervals). Similarly, the pace should be appropriate. The 5k runner will be doing short but fast intervals and the marathon runner longer intervals at a slightly slower pace.

Other factors that can be built into the interval session are the number of repetitions and the rest period and you should look at how long the running session will be when the warm-up and cool-down periods are included. Rest intervals should be walking or jogging.

The faster the effort, the longer the rest period should be. If you shorten the rest after flat-out effort, the pace will drop off rapidly. For intervals at <3k and 3–5k pace, two to three minutes is recommended between intervals but for slower intervals at 10k–half-marathon pace, 60–90 seconds is adequate (aerobic rather than anaerobic). Pace in intervals should be up to 80–90 per cent of your maximum, unless doing race simulations, which should be very infrequent.

Having decided on distance/pace/rest and repetitions, it is important that the intervals should be consistent, so that the given pace is maintained. However, more complicated interval patterns can be used. Any sort of intervals can be built into a run, either time or distance based and at variable paces and with different numbers of repetitions. Most sports watches can be programmed to create interval sessions, or you can use a stopwatch or gym timer. You can vary the rest period as above. If you live in a built-up area with streetlights, you can build your intervals around numbers of lamp posts, which is easier than fiddling with watches, as lamp posts are supposed to be 40m apart. Sometimes use unstructured intervals, not pre-planned: this is a bit like fartleks. You can also vary the stride length and cadence (step rate).

Fartlek training, developed by Gosta Holmer, represents a more free-form type of intervals (*fartlek* means 'speed play' in Swedish), where the intervals may vary in duration, distance and pace. This does not rely on watches and you should go by the feel. You should not stop to rest or walk in a fartlek but continue running at all times. Fartleks may be more akin to races, where your pace will not be constant – speeding up to pass someone, slowing down on an uphill segment and so on. It is useful discipline not to be a slave to your GPS watch and learn to feel how fast you are going and what effort it takes – you can go back and analyse what your watch has recorded afterwards. Fartleks are ideal for off-road interval training.

You can use terrain to vary the intervals. Consider using surges and strides in your regular runs, particularly long runs. When running long distances, it is easy to settle into a very fixed and limited stride pattern. You can improve muscular usage by doing random short surges, with an increase in pace, as you would if overtaking someone. You should also change your stride length for a period.

Like all training, it is the quality of the effort not the quantity that contributes to a positive training effect. Older runners may need to adapt intervals.

Hill sprints

Running intervals up hills is excellent training, and excellent for improving running form, as inevitably you will need to shorten your stride length. Always ensure that you have had a five- to ten-minute easy run to warm up before starting, and equally a cool-down run after. You can use any pattern of intervals on hills as you would on the flat. You can vary the recovery: walk back to the start, jog or run.

While hill sprints are useful training, whether you want to run uphill in races is debatable: it is more energy efficient to power-walk.

Downhill running

People assume that running downhill will be easy, after all gravity is pulling you down, isn't it? Actually running (not walking or jogging) downhill is harder and causes more problems than running uphill, as the quads have to work really hard when lengthening, not shortening. After a while this will become quite uncomfortable. You will also find that pain around the hips develops, as other muscles around the hips are doing the same. If you plan on running well in hilly country, practising running downhill

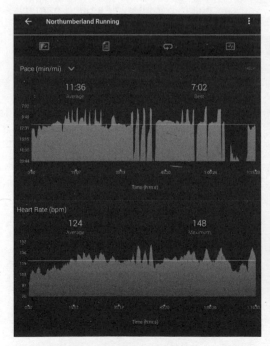

A typical fartlek interval session on the back of a tempo run. The distance/speed of the intervals is varied.

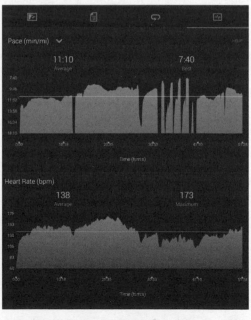

Hill sprints incorporated into a longer run. Recovery can be a walk/jog downhill.

at reasonable speeds is an essential part of training. You can incorporate downhill running into your hill intervals.

Avoid the tendency to lean back, which will increase your risks of slipping and stay light and balanced on the feet. When you see the fastest runners going downhill on trails, their feet barely seem to touch the ground as they fly down.

Types of runs including longer runs

Even your long runs need to have a purpose. Is it for recovery, is it an easy run or a tempo run? Try to choose interesting routes, as part of the knack of coping with long runs is mental distraction.

The easy run should be done at a comfortable pace that allows you to have a conversation – this will usually be one to two minutes per mile slower than your fastest pace and need not be that long. It can be used as recovery after harder sessions or races. The tempo or threshold run should be faster and the aim is to go at a pace that relies on aerobic metabolism in the muscles, but is not so fast that the muscles switch to anaerobic metabolism, where you start building up lactate in the muscle. This is usually going to be about 30 seconds per mile slower than your fastest 5k pace. It is not an all-out effort, but you will

> ## 'Try to choose interesting routes, as part of the knack of coping with long runs is mental distraction'

struggle to talk. This should be between 20–45 minutes at least once per week.

You should also consider a long run, of at least 60–90 minutes, but longer, up to three hours, if you are training for a marathon. This will be at the same pace as the easy run and the distance is less important than the time – this is about time on feet. The 60–90 minute mark is the point at which glycogen stores will be exhausted and muscles will switch to fat burning. This is crucial training if you plan to enter longer events. Preventing yourself from hitting the wall requires the muscles to have been adapted to switch to burning fat, and the only way that you can achieve this is by doing longer runs. These runs will give you the opportunity to practise in-run nutrition and hydration strategies and find out what works best for you.

Walk-run

People make the mistake of believing that if you have entered a run, you have to run! Particularly for those starting out, using walk-run can mean you do better than if you tried to run continuously. Walking (briskly, not ambling) is an efficient form of locomotion, particularly uphill. If you watch the most experienced trail and mountain runners, they all walk sections of their races, almost always the uphill sections (and will use running poles so they can support their legs).

You can do the same in road races too. Be disciplined about it and set intervals for running and walking, for example run for five minutes and walk for one minute: you may need to be flexible the longer a race goes on and depending on the terrain. Use the walk phase for eating/drinking.

In long races, periods of walking change the way you use the muscles and will help stretch out some of the stiffness that accumulates. Remember to relax and shake out the upper body, arms and neck.

Back-to-back runs

It is useful to incorporate back-to-back runs in your training, that is running on consecutive days or even two runs in a day. The purpose here is to learn how to run on tired legs. To begin with, make sure that you are already coping with your regular training schedule. The second run should be short to begin with, while you assess how it feels. Timetable your rest day after the back-to-back runs. Gradually you can increase the mileage of the second run. This will help if you plan multi-day events. Make sure you fuel and hydrate properly before, during and after each run. Monitor the effects of this closely, to make sure you are not overtraining.

Two runs in a day

Elite runners will often have two runs in a day. This does have training benefits, but average runners need to be cautious. One run should be short and fast and the other long and slow. The order can be varied. The total distance probably should be no more than you would normally run as a single run. This approach may be suitable for those with full-time jobs, who do not have time to do a long run in the week but can fit in a short run before work and one after work. Ensure that you do not omit the recovery.

PERIODISATION

Periodisation is planning your running training around your overall goals and major events. It is not helpful or effective to continue to train at the same level of intensity all the time. Periodisation requires a degree of planning ahead. Even for recreational runners, a degree of planning is essential for both enjoyment and performance.

Interestingly, one of the best books on periodisation of training by Karp (*see*

Resources) starts not with the training but with rest and recovery, which makes the point that good training is not all about how fast you train or how many miles you run, but how much time you allow the body for rest and recovery. To progress, each 'stress' must be followed by sufficient time for the body to adapt to the new stress. Failure to allow sufficient time for adaptation leads to exhaustion and failure to adapt (over-training). This theory also underpins the need to increase the training stress: doing the same training over and over does not improve the performance of recreational runners or high-performance elite athletes. When you go for your training runs think about how you can mix the training up: add a few hill reps, some intervals, fartleks, mix trail and road (trail is good for improving balance and co-ordination and is less hard on the feet).

Periodisation has been around since the 1960s and is usually divided into three or four periods. The first period usually lasting for a year is called the macrocycle and this is divided into shorter periods of between six and twelve weeks, referred to as the mesocycles. Each week within the mesocycle is referred to as the microcycle. The first step is to identify your major goal or goals for the year and then work backwards. This will be the A target: other races will be used as part of the build-up to the A race, referred to as the B and C races. Having identified the major target, training can be plotted backwards in time.

BASIC PERIODISATION

- Macrocycle – usually a plan for a year, covering key race targets
- Mesocycle – periods of training over six to twelve weeks (base, build, pre-competition and peak/race)
- Microcycle – usually each week's training plan

> *'Remember that as you age, the warm-up before training needs to be increased'*

There will usually be four distinct mesocycles phases before the A target, referred to as base, build, pre-competition and peak (the race). There also needs to be a rest/recovery phase after the main race. Intermediate races will form part of the training programme, aiming to deliver particular targets, for example speed or endurance.

Periodisation can be complex, with different models advised. This can include linear, reverse linear, block and undulating. The first two really apply to highly competitive runners, where there are a limited number of key events for which they are preparing. Undulating periodisation is what most of us do, mainly because life is like that: your job interferes, holidays, illness, the need to be ready for multiple races (although you can use races as training for a big event). Even if your periodisation is undulating, try to keep a clear plan of the eventual goal.

The base phase of training is designed to build endurance. The build phase will include strength and conditioning training, hill running, tempo runs and interval training with the intervals targeted around the event race distance. The pre-competition phase is accompanied by a reduction in training volume but more pace-specific practice, so hard runs with more recovery runs. In the peak or race phase all the hard work of the training should have been completed and you should aim to reduce all but the volume and intensity training to a degree which will keep your fitness level, avoid overtraining and keep you fresh for race day. This is often known as the pre-race taper. Over how long and by how much that should be done is again very individual.

Each weekly microcycle needs to have a range of different activities. Training needs to be mixed up to prevent boredom and to give the body chance to recover. There should be at least one rest day per week and for older runners this may need to be increased. Whatever other training pattern you use, it is worth making sure that over the course of the year there are longer breaks from training.

The purpose of any type of training programme is to optimise the training load and make sure that it is appropriate to the goals. You may find that some GPS sports watches will monitor your training load and give you suggestions for activities each day.

It is of course possible to train too much and the overtraining syndrome is recognised by sports medicine and will be discussed Chapter 9.

CIRCUIT TRAINING

Circuit training can be any type of exercise, for example running drills, sprints, bodyweight

> *'Persistent fatigue and/or raised resting pulse rate can be signs of overtraining: reducing training and taking more rest days is essential'*

exercises, HIIT and weight circuits, or indeed a combination. Each exercise can be done either for a fixed time or number of repetitions, followed by a rest period, which should be half the duration of the exercise phase. The shorter the rest period, the harder the circuit. In between each completed circuit there should be a longer break (several minutes) before the next cycle.

Many recommended exercises, especially bodyweight, are 'compound' exercises that exercise multiple muscle groups. For example, if you do a press-up (properly), you are working the muscles of the shoulder girdle, pectoral muscles, biceps and triceps, core (holding your back and abdomen straight) and leg muscles. Remember, a muscle does not have to be moving to be working: it may be contracting to hold the body in a particular position. The best example is the plank, where nothing is moving, but lots of muscles are working very hard.

There is clear evidence from research that circuit training, where the circuits are correctly designed, can increase VO_2 max and also improve lactate tolerance. Both of these will obviously be helpful to your running.

If you are designing your own circuits, you need to include elements of work for the arms, legs, core and cardiovascular system. Circuits can be predominantly aerobic, anaerobic (for example sprints, explosive exercises such as jumps or heavy weights) or a combination of the two. Incorporating both aerobic and anaerobic exercises into the same circuit is helpful. Alternating between upper and lower body exercises is harder and increases energy expenditure as the blood flow to muscles has to rapidly change. Mixing bodyweight circuits with runs (sprints) also adds difficulty. Make sure you vary the exercises; doing the same ones repeatedly will not lead to any progression. Changing the exercises provides new adaptive stress, as muscles are worked in a different way or in different combinations. If you are doing weight-based

exercise, there should be a slow increase in the weight.

Doing exercises in a series rather than sequentially is harder too. So, if you have a circuit of six different exercises and you are going to do the circuit three times, you can either go through all six exercises in sequence and then rest and repeat twice more, or you can do each exercise in the circuit three times, then move on to the next exercise and do this once. You have done the same number of exercises and taken the same time. The advantage of the latter is that the three repetitions of the same exercise means that there is less rest for the muscles involved in that exercise. This provides a stronger adaptive stress and gets you used to working with tired muscles.

Whatever type of running you plan, a strong core is essential. Particularly useful exercises are planks (all variations), press-ups, sit-ups, leg lowers and flutter kicks. Use of bands to do band walks, squats, hip extensions and other exercises is extremely valuable.

You do not need lots of fancy equipment to do circuit training. While you can join a fitness class and it is very helpful to have an instructor show you what to do, it is possible to do simple exercises at home. Flanders' *Cell Workout* (*see* Further Reading) describes a whole range of bodyweight exercises that can be carried out in a small space, and there is plenty of help online. You can obtain simple weights such as dumbbells, kettlebells and bands and these do not need to be expensive. For starters, large tins of beans make quite good hand weights.

Circuit training and any type of strength and conditioning should be built into your training programme, not necessarily in addition to running, but replacing a run session.

HIIT

HIIT is high intensity interval training (*see* Further Reading for details of Driver's basic introduction and a detailed guide by

Geissbuhler). It is important to recognise that HIIT is a concept of training and that any type of exercise (running, cycling, swimming, any type of circuit) can be done in the form of HIIT.

There is quite a lot of evidence that short bursts of high intensity activity, with rests between, can be as beneficial to fitness (muscular and cardiovascular) as continuous slower activity. This is an example of the adage that it is quality not quantity that matters. The total duration of activity can be quite short and still lead to measurable improvement over time. This type of approach to training is useful for the time-poor runner, as even short periods of 15–30 minutes can maintain or improve muscular and cardiovascular fitness if repeated regularly.

HIIT is an integral part of strength and conditioning training. Like all training, there needs to be evidence of progression over time: just doing the same exercises over and over will not lead to improvement. This can be through varying the exercises, adding or increasing weights and changing the intervals for exercise and rest. Aerobic HIIT circuits (mixed running and speed bodyweight exercises) will increase the VO_2 max quite significantly over time. Like all forms of exercise, you should have a proper dynamic warm-up before starting and a proper cool-down afterwards, each of five to ten minutes.

The top photograph shows the correct posture for a plank, whereas the lower photograph shows a poor posture which will be seen if core strength is weak.

The photo on the left shows a band squat and the one on the right shows a band extension. Stepping with bands around the ankles is extremely valuable (forwards, backwards and sidewards). Inexpensive bands can be bought online or in running shops. Different strength resistance bands are available, with black usually having the highest resistance.

Basic equipment for home circuit training. Left to right: a medicine ball (with or without handles), a roll-out wheel and some bands provide a basic kit; dumbbells are available in various weights and can be used to add weight in dynamic exercises (step-ups, jumping/running on the spot), as well as for arm exercises; kettlebells are extremely useful both for arm and leg exercises (kettlebell swings, squat with kettlebell and overhead push).

It is crucial to understand, from the perspective of having adequate rest and allowing the body to adapt to training stress, the HIIT sessions are not just an add-on session on top of a high mileage training schedule but should replace some of the running. Limiting HIIT to once or twice a week is sensible, when done as part of an overall training programme that incorporates running and strength training as well.

STRENGTH AND CONDITIONING

Strength and conditioning (S&C) training over-laps to a degree with circuit training but can also include specifically lifting weights. There is an informative guide by Nick Grantham (*see* Further Reading) but I have listed other resources as well.

There is a general acceptance among most running coaches now that regular strength and conditioning benefits overall performance and helps to prevent injuries. However, there is no evidence that strength training makes endur-ance runners go faster.

It breaks up the run training with something different. It can include circuit training, using either bodyweight or equipment, and strength training, lifting weights. The aim is to improve muscular power, neuromuscular co-ordination, strengthen soft tissues, prevent injuries and address well-known muscular weaknesses that negatively impact running performance, such as weak core strength or gluteal muscles.

Recommendations on exercise programmes may follow from a full gait and running style assessment. Any weight-based training has sig-nificant technical elements and you should ensure that you are taught how to do exercises properly by a qualified coach. Bodyweight training is simpler and requires no specific equipment. It is usually fairly easy to follow from the internet, books or DVDs. The *Runner's World* website gives a basic selection of key exercises. Choose a selection of four to eight exercises and either do a fixed number of rep-etitions or do 30–40 seconds on with 15–20s seconds' rest (it is usual to have a 2:1 ratio of exercise to rest) before moving to the next exercise. Do your chosen circuit twice. However, all exercises, even bodyweight, need to be done correctly for maximum benefit and to prevent injury.

Care needs to be taken when scheduling S&C training, particularly weight-based exer-cises targeting the lower body, as these can impair maximal running performance for up to 48 hours. When very fit it is possible to do strength and running on the same day but this is not recommended for average runners. You should view the workout as equivalent to a moderate intensity run and adjust your sched-ule accordingly. You should aim for one or two workouts per week. The aim over time with weight-based training (as with all training) is gradually over weeks or months to increase the load. When lifting weights, each set of repeti-tions needs to have a significant rest period of two to three minutes. The recommendation is to use heavy weights and concentrate on explosive power. Jump-based exercises are also recommended. However, if you have problems with the joints in the lower legs, you should avoid jump-based exercises.

Runners who will benefit most from S&C training are those have been injured, those with muscular imbalances, those who have a rela-tively low weekly mileage (for example those who have started running and are still building up endurance) and older runners, who will be losing speed and muscle power. Of course, for most people who run, the main reasons are to get fit and stay fit and to enjoy social interaction, not to become single-minded elite

> *'There is a general acceptance among coaches now that regular strength and conditioning benefits overall performance and helps to prevent injuries'*

runners, although some people surprise themselves and progress to elite levels. For the rest of us, having a varied training programme makes good sense. Overall, the science shows that elite runners benefit very little from cross-training, but average runners do benefit a lot.

There is a bewildering array of advice available, often contradictory. I have included my favourite books and websites in the Resources section, but the bottom line is go to a qualified professional trainer at a gym, preferably one who is interested and familiar with exercises for runners.

CROSS-TRAINING

Cross-training is valuable for a number of reasons:

- You can improve cardiovascular fitness without stressing your running muscles/joints, for example by using HIIT
- It enables you to build in exercise sessions to target weak muscles, such as gluteal muscles
- It prevents boredom setting in
- It is helpful if you have injuries that prevent you running, or when the weather is so foul that running isn't possible
- It can help prevent overuse injuries
- It can improve mental health and social interaction

As well as running, it is important for overall fitness to incorporate S&C and HIIT-based sessions. Other outdoor activities are also beneficial, such as recreational cycling, hiking and other sports. Be aware however that other sports including cycling may use very different muscles, and while they give you a break from running may not necessarily improve running fitness.

Cycling can give the same cardiovascular and metabolic benefits but without the impact stress on muscle and tendons. You need to travel three times as far on a bike as you would run to get the same cardiovascular effect. Using a bike on a turbo trainer in winter is a useful way of maintaining cardiovascular fitness when the roads are too icy to run safely, or you can buy expensive static bikes linked to web systems (such as Peloton) or do it as part of a fitness class (spinning). Be aware that running straight after cycling hard is difficult, as triathletes will recognise. Other alternative forms of exercise to consider for cross-training include indoor rowing, elliptical steppers, vertical steppers and treadmills (the belts are sprung so the impact effect is less).

OFF-ROAD TRAINING

Even if your main focus is road running, it is beneficial and fun to run off-road. There is less delayed onset muscle soreness after trail runs compared to road runs, due to variations in cadence and stride length (more muscles are being used). Overall impact effect on joints will be similar though, as your weight is the biggest determinant of this. It is important to have appropriate footwear if you are venturing off-road, to give grip and reduce the risk of falls and injury. Running off-road is harder than road running, so training mileage can be reduced. Running in mud is particularly hard. You need to practise both uphill and downhill running. Strides will necessarily be shorter and you need to practise balance exercises in your circuit training. You can do interval training, but because of uneven terrain, this is more likely to be of the random fartlek type. The eccentric exercise of muscles in downhill running means that the quads will hurt more. Practise, if possible, on all types of terrain.

Running on uneven ground means that it is quite difficult to get into a steady rhythm. You may also find yourself sliding around and moving in a very uneven way. It is important in training exercises to improve the muscle controlling lateral and twisting movements (side hops, side lunges, Russian twists). Band walks are particularly useful for improving the function of the inner thigh muscles, which are very important in controlling sideways movement.

If you live near the sea and there are sandy beaches, running on sand is excellent training, as it is harder work. Beware that, as most beaches slope down to the sea, prolonged periods of running in the same direction can lead to hip and knee pain because you are constantly running at a right-angle to the slope. Change direction at regular intervals. If there are sand dunes, running up and down is even harder work, and good training! Be aware that sand dunes are important wildlife habitats and play an important role in limiting flooding. If possible, use well-established pathways. Sand dunes may have steps – these

also are an excellent training aid. If the beach is rocky, rocks under water at high tide may be extremely slippery. Make sure you check tides and know that your route will not mean you get cut off when the tide comes in. Running barefoot can also be extremely good for strengthening the feet but take care for hidden objects in the sand.

Training off-road gives you the opportunity to work out which trail shoes work best in given conditions and to practise the use of poles. It is also worth getting used to running with a loaded race pack before you try using one in a race.

If you intend to train in wild country, with high hills/fells, make sure that you have checked the weather forecast and are aware of the potential for different weather on fell

Beaches are excellent for training! Sand dunes are useful, but stick to paths. Beaches always have a slope and this can cause hip problems, so switch directions to balance the effect.

tops, as well as the temperature drop as you climb. Even for training runs, you should be carrying appropriate safety equipment, food, drink and extra clothing including waterproofs. Make sure someone knows where you have gone and how long you expect to be. This means planning a rough route before departing and sticking to it. Hill walking is very good training for off-road and mountain running. Make sure this is done at a reasonable speed and practise using poles for climbing and descending.

RUNNING WITH POLES

It is important to learn how to use these properly. Running with poles takes some practice and tends to be one cycle with the arms to two with the legs. Using poles requires good upper body and core strength.

Be careful of other runners when using poles, to prevent injury or tripping. In particular, be careful on narrow paths and at stiles/gates. When carrying them on race packs, make sure the points are down. If mounting them horizontally, be aware that the points may stick out, so give fellow runners a wide berth. It is your responsibility to know where the tips of your poles are at all times. Loading and unloading poles from race packs and assembling them takes a while, but using them will save time on your climb.

The use of two poles when on rough uphill climbs is a huge benefit; equally coming down steep ascents, poles correctly used can provide extra balance, but getting the tip of a pole caught in narrow cracks can unbalance you. When descending, remember your body posture is crucial: you should be leaning forward. Poles can help. Leaning back increases the risk of slips and falls. Streams can be vaulted with the use of poles. For ultra events, spells of power walking (Nordic walking) with poles can be useful as a way of making good progress while conserving energy and resting the running muscles.

Beware that not all races permit the use of poles. Check race regulations.

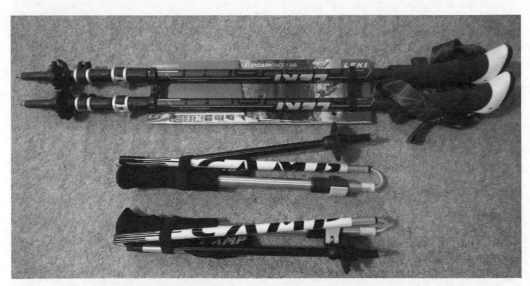

Telescopic running poles (top) with knurled knob to tighten each length (can come loose). Z-fold poles (bottom) which are bulkier but once assembled stay at the correct length. Materials range from carbon fibre (most expensive and lightest), through titanium (less expensive and still lightweight) to aluminium (cheapest and prone to distortion if force applied).

YOGA FOR RUNNERS

Runners can get quite stiff: it is after all a very repetitive exercise. As our lives are increasingly sedentary, we are getting less mobile. Being sedentary increases posture problems with neck and back and leads to weak core muscles. Because the hips and knees are continuously flexed, the hamstring muscles are shortened and easily get tight. Yoga-based exercises can be very helpful in this setting to increase mobility and deal with tight muscles, especially on rest/recovery days. Yoga exercises are complex multi-joint and multi-muscle exercises and often include a strong element of balance training, which is excellent, especially for trail runners.

Yoga training should also include breathing control, which can contribute to improved lung function and is obviously beneficial to runners.

Yoga also includes elements of mindfulness, useful for mental health issues and helps develop calmness. It may also help in coping with the pressures of races, particularly longer races, in particular dealing with negative feelings and coping with discomfort. Yoga can therefore be usefully incorporated into the training schedule as a form of cross-training and for post-race recovery. In its fullest form, yoga is a complex mind-body training. Embracing all parts of yoga may be valuable to some people, but even if you don't want to delve deeply, utilising well-established simple yoga exercises will still be a benefit.

There are a lot of internet resources for yoga and an excellent book by Christine Felstead (*see* Further Reading). This book gives detailed descriptions of yoga poses and specifically how they are of benefit. Research the best exercises or better still go to a qualified trainer – not all exercises are suitable for every runner and underlying joint and muscle conditions may contraindicate some (*see* Resources). It is quite possible to injure yourself by doing the wrong type of yoga exercises or doing them incorrectly. If you experience pain or discomfort while doing an exercise, alter the posture or stop the exercise. Try to do yoga exercise once or twice a week and certainly as part of the recovery after hard runs/races.

> *'Yoga exercises are complex multi-joint and multi-muscle exercises and often include a strong element of balance training, which is excellent, especially for trail runners'*

TRAINING FOR HEAT, COLD AND WET

If you are planning events in the heat or cold, it is important to include appropriate exposure training. Running in extreme environments is beyond the scope of this book, but if you are planning on running something like the Marathon du Sables or the Antarctic marathon, seek experienced professional advice. Even in more temperate climates such as the UK, very hot or cold weather conditions can catch unprepared runners out. Ensure that you have practised running in the heat or cold if possible before the event and that you have the correct clothing and equipment, even when training.

Running in the heat

Heat will increase the rate of sweating as the body tries to maintain the body temperature. Working muscles generate heat and this has to be disposed of. Blood flow will increase to the skin to facilitate this. The impact of temperature is also modified by the humidity. In high humidity, sweat will evaporate slowly and therefore there will be little cooling effect, but when the humidity is low the cooling effect will be greater. Evaporation of sweat will be enhanced in the breeze so the higher the windspeed, the greater the cooling effect. As you get fitter the body learns to sweat more as an adaptation to keep the core temperature stable.

Choosing appropriate lightweight clothing to run in the heat is essential. Choose pale colours as these do not heat up in sunlight. This is one reason why it is so annoying that men's technical running gear is usually any colour as long as it is black (with apologies to Henry Ford). Materials should ideally be technical high wicking to prevent sweat-soaked material causing chafing or blisters. All areas that are exposed to the sun should be covered with an appropriate sunscreen with the minimum SPF of 30 or if it is a longer race, SPF 50. Suddenly switching to thin mesh vests when you have been wearing T-shirts means that there are areas of the body which will have had little sun exposure and may burn. Mesh fabrics mean that UV light can penetrate and cause sunburn under clothing. Some manufacturers give an SPF for their clothing.

If you are running regularly for long periods in bright sunshine, wear sunglasses or Reactolite prescription glasses. Polarising sunglasses will reduce glare from water and sand. Breathable caps also reduce glare, enhance evaporation of sweat from the head and stop sweat running down into the eyes. A neck protector attached to the cap is also wise. Running in sand means that shoes and socks will fill with sand which is abrasive and will cause blisters over long runs: using gaiters attached to the shoes helps reduce this.

If you are training in hot weather, aim to do runs either early in the morning or the late afternoon or evening. Remember only mad dogs and Englishmen go out in the midday sun! However, if you know that you'll be doing a race during the hottest part of the day you should include this in your training runs. Running in the heat will slow you down significantly and you should be prepared to adjust your pace accordingly. Every 3°C rise in temperature will slow you down by about 20–30 seconds per mile.

You should ensure that you are fully hydrated before setting off on your run and then aim to drink regularly while running. Practise being comfortable running while carrying adequate fluid. This can either be in a hydration bladder in your backpack or via flasks carried on the front of the race pack.

You can get race bum bags which have the capacity for carrying smaller quantities of fluid but these may not be adequate for very long races. It is best to sip steadily; the gut has a reduced

CHECKLIST FOR RUNNING IN HOT WEATHER

- If possible, run early in the morning or in the evening
- Plan route to maximise shade and run into any wind for additional cooling
- Wear light-coloured clothing
- Use a cap and sunglasses to protect eyes
- Use appropriate sunscreen (SPF 30–50)
- Take sufficient drinks and extra salt if necessary
- If doing a race where hot weather will be expected, train in heat if possible
- Expect to run more slowly (20–30s per mile slower for every 3°C rise in temperature)

The top photo shows a race pack with a hydration bladder. This has insulation around it to keep it cool and prevent body heat from warming it up. The feed tube runs from the base and is held on the front chest straps with a bite valve. The lower photo shows a lightweight mesh race vest with two soft water flasks held on the front.

capacity to absorb food and fluids during runs. If you are planning very long training runs in the heat then consider a drive round beforehand, dropping off top-up fluid. If possible, avoid running on tarmac or concrete and plan a route that includes running on grass or trails, preferably in the shade. Choosing a route so that you are running into the wind on the return will help with cooling when you are hottest.

How much you need to drink when running in the heat is contentious. Elite athletes can cope with drinking less, but normally recommendations for consumption vary between 300–800ml per hour, although 800ml may be far too much unless the temperature is extreme. The best guide is drink to thirst, but be aware that the sensation of thirst becomes less acute as you get older (*see* Chapter 4 for detailed advice on hydration).

Running in heat and sun can cause a number of problems. Dehydration will manifest as deteriorating performance and fatigue, together with dizziness and eventually fainting. Core body temperature will rise. You should stop running, find shade, cool yourself (icepacks to neck and head) and restore fluid with isotonic electrolyte drinks, consumed slowly, to give the gut time to absorb them. Restart the run only when symptoms are subsiding. If symptoms do not improve, seek help.

Hyponatraemia is a drop in the sodium level in the blood from either excessive salt loss through sweating or excessive water intake, or both. Symptoms include headache, dizziness, disorientation, muscle twitching and eventually fitting and loss of consciousness. Treatment is a medical emergency. In the early stages, it can be difficult to distinguish between dehydration and hyponatraemia. Avoid drinking large volumes of water, without salt. Muscle cramps affecting abdominal or leg muscles are a sign of salt depletion as well as dehydration.

Heatstroke occurs when there is a combination of extreme exertion and dehydration leading to an uncontrolled rise in core body

> '*If you have to stop for any reason, the body will start cooling immediately and it is important to have appropriate clothing*'

temperature. Headache, nausea, vomiting, rapid pulse and disorientation will occur. This is a medical emergency and rapid cooling and rehydration under medical supervision is required.

Running in the cold

Winters in the UK are not usually exceptionally cold. For an averagely cold winter, it is worth having good thermal tops and tights and windproof/waterproof jackets and over-trousers. Warmer socks are good. While one frequently sees elite runners out in vests and shorts in winter races, this is not advisable for average runners. If you have to stop for any reason, the body will start cooling immediately and it is important to have appropriate clothing. Wet cold weather is worse than dry.

Beware of putting on too much clothing and over-heating. The rule of thumb is to dress for a temperature 10–20°C higher than the air temperature. If you are hanging around for any length of time for a race to start, ideally have something warm to wear that can be left at the start with family/friends or with the event organisers (baggage drop). Learning about layering is crucial. Air is trapped between the layers and is a very good insulator. Make sure the bottom layer is a long-sleeved wicking fabric.

Merino wool is an excellent and sustainable material for tops, underwear and socks as it is extremely warm for its weight and retains insulation properties even when wet. The combination yarns now available mean that it wicks sweat reasonably. Synthetic materials also perform well.

When running or walking in mountains, you need to take into consideration that temperature will drop with increasing altitude. It may be warm and sunny at the bottom of the mountain, but very cold at the top with a much higher windspeed: take extra clothing!

A three-layer system is usually advised, with a base layer, a mid layer and an outer shell (windproof/waterproof). This approach works well for the body but is harder for legs. Remember that the muscle in the legs will be generating a lot of heat as you run, so thinner is better. If the temperature is really cold (down to or below freezing) thermal clothing is advised. As well as thermal tops and bottoms look for thermal socks, beanies and gloves: you will lose 7–10 per cent of your heat through an

---

Temperature decrease with altitude:

6.5°C for every 1,000m or 2°C for every 1,000ft climbed

Calculating wind chill factor:

Multiply the wind speed (mph) by 0.7 and then subtract that from the air temperature

Example:

At a windspeed of 10mph and an air temperature of 10°C, perceived temperature is 10 -(10×0.7) = 3°C

If the windspeed increased to 20mph, perceived temperature would be -4°C!

unprotected head and probably more if you are bald.

When running on roads and pavements in winter in freezing conditions, beware of black ice. Ice may be a hazard even on trails, although there tends to be more grip. If you are running in snow or on ice, consider running shoes with integrated titanium studs in the outsole to provide grip. However, do not use these on roads without snow or ice as the studs will wear down quickly. An alternative is to get grips that fit over shoes such as Yaktrax or Black Diamond, or Icespike which you can screw into the soles of an old pair of trainers (*see* Resources). In loose, fresh snow, trail shoes with studs for mud will be fine.

Running in snow is fun, however if you are running on fells and mountains, be very aware of the possibilities of cornices developing. These are areas of snow extending out beyond the edge of the mountain, created by the wind. If you step on these, there will be no solid surface underneath you and the cornice may collapse. If you have not run in the mountains in the snow, get advice and training and preferably go with someone who is experienced (*see* Resources). There is a risk of snow blindness, which is due to light damage to the retina. Wear either good-quality sunglasses or snow goggles.

Hydration is still important even in cold weather, especially if it is cold and dry. Nutrition is also important as you will use more energy in cold weather. Running through snow is tiring, so adjust training runs accordingly.

If you are planning long winter runs, a bivvy sac and/or foil blanket are valuable additions. Also make sure you have food and fluid: a small lightweight insulated flask means that you can take a hot drink with you. Keep some of the food and drink for emergencies only. Beware of the windchill factor. In cold weather, higher winds mean that the perceived temperature is lower. A simple windchill calculator is available online (*see* Resources). Weather services in some UK national parks will provide information on windchill.

The main risk for winter running is hypothermia, when the core temperature drops (defined as below 35°C). As your body temperature falls, you will become more lethargic, the pulse rate will fall and eventually you will lose consciousness. Hypothermia will set in rapidly if you have to stop for any reason in sub-zero temperatures. This is a medical emergency. Ensure that you have extra layers to put on.

In freezing conditions batteries on mobile phones will go flat faster. Insulated pouches are available. Keep the phone close to your body to keep it warm and use it sparingly so there is plenty of charge available in emergencies. Better to have a separate camera and have waterproof lightweight maps.

Running in rain and wind

One of the things that puts people off running is the rain, especially in the winter. What you wear depends on the temperature, but essentially to stay reasonably dry you need a proper waterproof and breathable top.

You can decide whether you want to have waterproof overtrousers, but bear in mind that the rain will run off your waterproof top and soak into your shorts or leggings. You will most probably get wet feet and using Gore-Tex trainers doesn't really help as the water runs down your legs into the shoes and then can't escape. Best to just grin and bear the wet feet. If you know you are going to be out for a long period with wet feet, rubbing Vaseline into the feet beforehand prevents the skin from becoming waterlogged and therefore more likely to breakdown and blister. You can get waterproof socks, or merino socks are the best for keeping feet warm even if wet, as merino wool retains its insulation properties. Bridgedale have an excellent range of running socks (*see* Resources). Waterproof over-mitts can keep the hands dry and warm.

Being wet and cold is a bad combination, so investing in a decent jacket is money well

When running in heavy rain, make sure you have appropriate high-quality waterproof clothing and if off-road, shoes with a good grip as trails will become very slippery. Reproduced with permission from Lakeland Trails and photographed by James Kirby (who valiantly sat out in torrential rain to photograph the runners on the Hellvellyn Trail Race).

spent. The hoods on some jackets have peaks, but spectacle wearers may prefer a cap (with the jacket hood over the top) with a long brim to keep the rain off glasses. Make sure clothing and especially shoes are thoroughly dried after running. Stuffing shoes with newspaper helps remove the moisture.

If out on trails, paths may become very slippery with mud: use appropriate footwear with long studs for better grip. Paths may be washed out and rocky tracks will be very slippery. Tiny mountain streams may become raging torrents very quickly. Reduce your run speed appropriately.

Ensure that you are visible with appropriate clothing and lights. Remember on roads, drivers' vision will also be impaired, so take extra care.

Running in high winds is inadvisable (as well as being extremely hard work), especially in woodland. After storms, trees that have been damaged may still fall later and, interestingly, trees that have been pushed sideways may actually spring back upright without warning. If you are planning on using trails in open access forest managed by Forestry England, check the relevant website or Facebook page

'Ensure that you are visible with appropriate clothing and lights. Remember on roads, drivers' vision will also be impaired, so take extra care'

to see whether the trails are open. Equally on high ground, especially mountains, you may encounter unexpected extreme gusts which can lift you off your feet with no warning.

TRAINING FOR NIGHT RUNNING

Running at night will be inevitable at some times of the year. However, there are many races that now take place specifically at night, often in places where light pollution is minimal, so that you can really appreciate the stars on a clear night. For ultra events, a major part of the run may be done at night. It will take up to 20–30 minutes for full night vision to develop after moving from light to dark. If you are dark adapted and someone shines their head torch in your face, it will take a considerable time for the night vision to return fully. Therefore, run slowly for the first twenty minutes until your night vision is established. You get a better view at night by not looking directly at an object, but looking slightly away from it.

Running at night requires attention to clothing (reflective), head torches and also requires you to consider your safety. Choose your route carefully, preferably where there are other people and stay in lit areas wherever possible. Stay in open ground where you can see any hazards. Carry a phone and/or personal alarm. Make sure someone knows where you are going and when to expect you back. Preferably run with someone.

Your perceptions will be different at night. It will seem as if you are running faster than you are. Even on routes you know, objects will seem different and particularly if you are tired, your mind will start playing tricks. You will feel more alone. It is not unusual to feel more uneasy in woods at night, but woods can be very interesting, with night-time animals about such as badgers and foxes, and birds such as owls. It is especially wonderful to see barn owls, white shadows floating silently by.

CHECKLIST FOR RUNNING AT NIGHT

- Plan your route, preferably by running in the day and make a note of waymarkers, turn-points, hazards and so on
- Let someone know where you are going if running alone
- Wear hi-viz clothing
- Use a head torch
- Carry spare batteries or an emergency head torch if planning to be out for a while
- Take a phone

The major issues for night running are vision and the ability to see obstacles well in advance. There is also a need to run in a light and balanced way so that it is easier to avoid obstacles. For most, night running will be on roads and pavements, but even with street lighting it is advisable to wear a head torch to illuminate the ground about 6ft ahead, which will give you sufficient time to take evasive action. Reduce pace to ensure safety.

Some people do find running with head torches quite disconcerting as the pattern of light jigs up and down and can cause nausea, similar to seasickness. In this case using a chest harness with an LED torch at the front and red LED at the back is helpful.

You should also check how long the torch will maintain its illumination at a given power. As runners' head torches are LED based, their burn times are usually more than adequate for anything other than extreme night-time running. When doing long night-time runs it is important to take either spare batteries, a small back-up head torch or have a very large battery to start with. Be aware that battery performance drops off sharply in cold weather, shortening the burn time. The burn time at -5°C is half that of the same battery at 20°C.

For off-road night running, the risks are magnified by the uneven surface and hazards such as rocks and tree roots. A decent head torch is a must. Any sort of night running requires you to pay more attention to navigation as it is much easier to miss regular landmarks for turns in the dark. It is not advisable to try running a trail for the first time at night. Better to run it in the day and make navigation notes that you can strap to your arm: turn points with the mileage from the start point or create a GPX file you can upload to your watch. However, it is wise not to become too reliant on electronic devices and lose the skills of proper navigation. If you are doing an organised event that involves night running, I would strongly advise plenty of night-time training runs to hone your skills.

SPECIFIC TRAINING POINTS FOR WOMEN

Women during their reproductive years have an added disadvantage for training and racing: their menstrual cycle, which means that performance will vary throughout the month. But there are also some advantages. Firstly, oestrogen is good at promoting muscles to burn fat, rather than rely on glycogen. This is a particular advantage for long runs. Women have more slow twitch fibres in their muscle and less fast twitch muscle fibres, which is a big help for long-distance running, as slow twitch muscle fibres are more resistant to fatigue.

'Pre-menstrual symptoms can have a major impact on ability to run and train'

Finally, women generally tolerate fatigue and discomfort better than men.

In the first half of the cycle when oestrogen is the dominant hormone, running will be easier, as oestrogen helps fat-burning. The second half of the cycle is dominated by progesterone: while this increases muscle glycogen (a benefit), it also increases the rate of breathing independent of exercise, which may make the effort of exercise seem greater. Body temperature is increased in this phase of the cycle, which makes running in the heat harder. Pre-menstrual symptoms can have a major impact on ability to run and train. However, as progesterone and oestrogen levels drop, body temperature and heart rate fall and the body's ability to metabolise carbohydrate improves. These changes can help performance. During a period, cramps may be limiting, although running can help some people. Heavy menstrual bleeding, especially with cramps, can obviously significantly hamper running.

Training needs to be adjusted to take these factors into account, a form of undulating periodisation. Women who run a lot will often stop menstruating, which does represent a deficiency of oestrogen and this has a long-term negative effect on bone density. Discussing this with your doctor is sensible. It is not all bad though – impact exercise such as running strengthens bones, provided that the diet contains adequate calcium and vitamin D. Being out in sunshine also promotes vitamin D synthesis in the skin.

For women who have regular periods, iron deficiency is a risk, which will have profound effects on running ability and increased fatigue. These are similar symptoms to overtraining, so difficult to diagnose without testing. Leafy green vegetables, tuna and red meats are the best sources of absorbable iron, but also almonds, figs, kidney beans, tofu and dark chocolate. Vitamin C helps the absorption of dietary iron but tea prevents its absorption. Iron absorption is impaired immediately after exercise. Taking too much iron as supplements isn't good either, so beware of the DIY route to supplements without professional advice and appropriate tests. If you are doing a lot of running, getting regular annual checks is wise. If you have been deficient in iron or anaemic, more frequent testing is advised.

Running and pregnancy

If you are an established runner when you become pregnant, there is no specific reason to stop running. Gynaecologists recommend exercise in pregnancy for 20–30 minutes a day, but it is a good idea to discuss exercise plans with health professionals. Other benefits from exercise in pregnancy include a reduced risk of gestational diabetes, pre-eclampsia and Caesarean section. If you have never run before pregnancy, this can be a difficult time to start.

Exercise in the first trimester can be limited by morning sickness and if you can't eat/drink properly then do not try running. The second trimester is usually better, although as the baby grows your centre of gravity will change, so take extra care when running on rough ground. Be prepared to run more slowly. Avoid getting too hot, as a seriously raised maternal body temperature may be associated with birth defects. Hydrate well, run in the coolest parts of the day and wear appropriate loose-fitting wicking clothing. Running becomes more difficult in the third trimester due to the size of the bump. Also, at this time the body starts producing the hormone relaxin which loosens ligaments, and this can lead to more pain around the hips and lower back and may increase the risk of ligament and tendon injury, especially if running on uneven ground.

After delivery, all the tissues are still very lax, so be cautious about exercise, especially strength exercises and running. Respond in the same way as you would if injured and build back up slowly. Fatigue will also be significant and if you are breastfeeding, this will also have an impact on fatigue, nutrition and hydration. If you have had a Caesarean section, the scar will take at least six weeks to heal on the surface, but the internal reconstruction will take the body much longer (up to six months to reach 75 per cent of its original strength) so seek advice on return to running/exercise from your GP and obstetrician.

Running and the menopause

The menopause is associated with significant hormonal changes. Running is certainly beneficial post-menopause as it will help maintain bone density. It is estimated that up to 20 per cent of the bone density is lost in the five to seven years after the onset of the menopause. Sustained aerobic exercise is deemed helpful by the Royal College of Obstetrics and Gynaecology for dealing with the side effects of the menopause (low mood, flushes, night sweats and disturbed sleep), although it is not a magical cure.

If you have been running before the menopause, there is no reason to stop. If you have not run before, running is a good choice for helping you cope. Post-menopausal women should also make sure that they undertake strength and resistance training, to maintain muscle function. Yoga is a valuable exercise supplement to maintain flexibility.

TRAINING FOR OLDER RUNNERS

Sadly, for all of us running performance declines with age, with a linear decline from age 45. After the age of 65–70 years the rate of decline increases sharply. Running economy doesn't change much but running gait changes with reduced stride length (cadence is maintained). The gait changes seem mainly to be due to changes in the joints and increasing stiffness in the tendons. The main joint affected is the ankle.

The reduction in VO_2 max is down to a decline in lung function, changes in the heart that reduce the amount of blood that the heart pumps out and a reduction in the oxygen-carrying capacity of the blood. Uptake of oxygen into tissues also declines with age.

The good news is that training slows the rate of decline. Muscle, heart and lung function is better maintained in older runners, compared to those who don't run. Remaining physically active also has important effects on maintaining cognitive function and neuro-muscular co-ordination, which will reduce the risks of falls. It is a myth that running causes arthritis – it may even help arthritis, and it reduces the risks of certain cancers, strokes, heart attacks, Alzheimer's disease, diabetes and high cholesterol.

You can reinvigorate your running as you age by getting a proper gait analysis. Gait often changes, perhaps influenced by past

---

'It is a myth that running causes arthritis – it may even help arthritis, and it reduces the risks of certain cancers, strokes, heart attacks, Alzheimer's disease, diabetes and high cholesterol'

---

injuries, which can contribute to increased joint and muscle pain and cause reduction in pace. I did this at a point when I thought that I might have to give up running altogether because of joint pains. A change in running style reduced the pain substantially and led to a significant improvement in race times, in fact rolling back the clock by about six years. Reviewing your shoes may be helpful: a more cushioned shoe may take some of the strain off ageing joints.

As part of gait re-evaluation, undertaking strength and conditioning training becomes increasingly important with age. Without this, muscle bulk and muscle function will gradually decline. Programmes need to be age-appropriate and designed by an experienced personal trainer, familiar with the needs of older runners.

In practical terms, it takes older runners longer to warm up than younger runners. I find I need twenty minutes of easy running before I feel fully up to speed. Interestingly my heart rate monitor agrees: for the first twenty minutes my pulse rate is high then when I feel ready to go, it drops. Older runners running in mixed-age group training sessions need to bear this in mind and should not allow themselves to be pushed into speedwork until they feel comfortably warmed up. Trying to compete with the younger runners is a fast track to muscle injury.

A very good book that reviews the science behind running in older populations plus inter-views with seriously good runners in the post-retirement age group (including those over 100) is Richard Askwith's *The Race against Time* (*see* Further Reading). This shows that age is no bar to performances that would not be a disgrace to a 30–40 year old. No single factor has been identified to account for why and how some individuals can continue to run at a high level into later life. There doesn't appear to be a par-ticular type of training that works best. All the runners agree that keeping running is the most important factor, along with enjoying every run.

TRAINING FOR THE DISABLED

This is a complex area, because of the wide range of factors. The principles of training are no different than for non-disabled runners. It is important for disabled runners to access a coach/trainer with relevant knowledge. Additional exercises may be required to deal with muscular imbalances, for example in cerebral palsy, and to work on balance and co-ordination. Training needs to focus on building up confidence and developing a supportive network of fellow runners. Like all activities, the mental approach determines the level of success. Goal setting in training is just as important and goals must be appropriate, realistic and achievable. Blind runners may be able to find companion runners who will run with them, often linked at the wrist. Being a companion runner is an art, as you have to be able to give a sensible commentary on upcoming hazards, especially for off-road running.

MENTAL TRAINING

People forget that running, especially long distances, has less to do with the legs and much more to do with the mind. Many studies have shown that the perception of fatigue during a run is a brain phenomenon that is designed to 'protect' the body. When you feel fatigue, the muscles are quite capable of carrying on (assuming you have done enough training). The best ultrarunners recognise this and focus on mind-training to overcome it.

The psychological process begins with goal setting. This has to be realistic and achievable, albeit challenging, within a sensible timeframe. If you have just started running, suggesting to yourself that you will get fit enough to run a marathon in three months is not going to happen without high risk of injury. You need your long-term goals (complete my first marathon in six months) and these will be achieved by a number of short-term goals (run 5k, run

10k, run a half-marathon and so on). Write goals down. Your training plan will be the route map to achieving your goals. Do not set vague goals such as 'I want to run further or faster' – be specific. If things aren't going well, be prepared to re-evaluate goals and reset them – there is nothing shameful about this.

Self-belief is crucial. This means developing the confidence that you have done the right training and that you can do the event. This comes from a number of sources: what you have done before, what you have seen others do, positive affirmation from yourself and from friends, family and coaches, and your perception of your strengths, weaknesses, ability to cope with fatigue and pain. Unsurprisingly, those with the most positive self-belief perform best and get the best results. Basically, if you really want to do something, you can and you will.

A major technique is distraction. This can be training your mind to think of other things, examining the countryside, listening to the birds, listening to music, although I am not a fan of wearing headphones when running on roads as you cannot hear potential hazards. Having a companion to talk to and share the experience with is valuable and improves motivation. I write my books in my head as I do my long runs. The trick is not to distract yourself so much that you become unaware of hazards.

Most techniques come under the heading of mindfulness in its widest sense. There has been increasing focus on mindful running, particularly to improve the beneficial effects of running on mental illness. Mindfulness means being more aware of the moment and more aware of your body. Learning to control your breathing is a part. Concentrate on relaxing your arms, neck and face, all of which tend to get tight during a run. Be cheerful: smile at people you meet and greet them (and not with a grunt). Stopping focusing on distance and pace will help. Learn to run to your RPE. Using mindful techniques helps you cope with the physical discomfort: you reach a point where

KEY ASPECTS OF MENTAL TRAINING IN RUNNING

- Set realistic goals and re-evaluate regularly
- Do not set vague goals
- Do not be afraid to alter your goals if circumstances change
- Believe in yourself
- Remain positive and use self-talk ('stop shuffling')
- Have a mantra to repeat
- Set mini-goals ('catch the next runner', 'push on to the next aid station')
- Use distraction techniques to cope with bad spells in a run
- Use imagery: break up a long race into a series of short distances that you know you can do easily. Imagine how great it will be to cross the finish line and get your medal
- Concentrate on relaxing breathing and shake out stiff muscles
- Avoid focusing on watch and pace
- Inadequate fuel/hydration will increase negative feelings: eat and drink

you are aware of it but it doesn't concern you. Concentrating on the immediate surroundings and not focusing on how much further you have to run is crucial for long races.

Like everything in life retaining a positive outlook is key. It is very easy on long runs to slip into a negative way of thinking. Psychologists often recommend having a positive mantra that you can repeat to yourself at tough points: 'I can do it'. Self-talk (in a positive way) is helpful: 'stop shuffling, pick up your feet, stand up, push now'. Self-talk can be instructional or motivational. It is important to pre-prepare for those difficult times in races when things seem to be going badly.

It is important to be able to assess situations accurately and evaluate symptoms such as pain, fatigue, dizziness and understand which symptoms can be overridden and which really are clear indications to stop.

Train yourself not to be a fair-weather runner, as not all your races will be in ideal conditions. This means not skipping training because it's raining, it's cold or the wind is blowing. This will develop the resilience to cope whatever the conditions.

Just as you taper your physical effort as part of your periodisation and preparation for a race, don't forget to taper mentally. This means cutting down on other things that will stress or tire you.

Imagery can be used to break up long races into sections. Most people running marathons for the first time think about how far 26 miles is when they get in their car and drive 26 miles, and then think they couldn't possibly run that far. The trick is to divide the distance into shorter blocks of 5–6 miles which you know you can do, by visualising your favourite run and imagining you are just running round this loop. When you get to the end you say, 'Well I have done that, I am sure I can do another 5-mile loop' and so on until the end. You are never running 26 miles – just 5-mile loops!

Do not underestimate the benefit from crowd support. When I ran the London Marathon (my first marathon), the noise for the last 5 miles was incredible and the positive energy from the crowd carried me on to the end. If you are planning to do a first major distance (half or full marathon or ultra) try to

'It is important to pre-prepare for those difficult times in races when things seem to be going badly'

enter one where there will be crowds of supporters. If you have done your test 20-miler successfully, you will be able to do the extra 6 miles with the energy from the crowd willing you on.

Another mental strategy that is important is training yourself not to follow the herd at the start. In many races, there may be lots of people who go off really fast and it is easy without discipline to get dragged along too quickly, an error that you may well pay for later in the race. Go at your pace – you will overtake the quick starters towards the end, when they start flagging. Remember the fable of the tortoise and the hare.

At the end of the day, in the same way that you train your body to cope, you must train your mind and develop the mental resilience to cope when the going gets tough. It may also explain why, the longer the distance, the more women perform as well as or better than men. The female brain seems to be able to cope as well or better with the mental requirements of extreme running (sorry blokes). They also tolerate fatigue better.

Rightly, much has been made of the benefits of running for mental health. Benefits accrue in a number of ways: a sense of achievement, improved social interaction, getting outside, the runner's high (production of natural euphoriant chemicals in the brain), improved self-image (weight loss, increased muscular tone).

OVERTRAINING: LESS IS MORE

I have direct experience of overtraining: after training hard to run the London Marathon, I entered too many races and didn't have enough rest. I had to take over a year off, with running cut down to a minimum, to facilitate recovery.

Once you get into running, and enjoy the buzz, there is often a desire to improve and push yourself harder and further. Just doing the same level of activity (intensity and volume) will not lead to improvement in either pace or endurance. However, it is quite easy to do too much. There is a very fine line between increasing the training and over-training and sometimes you do not realise until it is too late. Ensuring that you have a proper training/racing plan is a good place to start and making sure that you record your training and race performance. If things are going wrong, you have a starting point to evaluate the problem. Make sure that your training has proper periodisation, as this will build in phases when the intensity is reduced to allow for proper recovery.

Pointers to overtraining are increasing fatigue that does not resolve, an increase in minor muscular niggles which take longer to recover, disturbed sleep, lethargy and mood disturbance, poor appetite and an increased resting pulse rate. There is often an increase in minor infections. Motivation will drop. Libido will decrease. In women, periods may stop. The pulse rate response to exercise is also increased. Your best pace will be slower and your race times will fall away (unexplained underperformance syndrome – UUPS). Many sports watches now have fitness trackers, based on algorithms related to your heart rate vs pace and resting heart rate. These will give you early warning that things are not as they should be. Use these as an adjunct to listening to what your body is telling you.

Over-racing is another cause. This applies particularly to endurance runners doing marathon or ultra events. After major events, training must be stopped for a reasonable period: a recommended rest period is one day for every hour of running. For a five-hour marathon that's five days and for a 24-hour race, that's no running for 24 days. Rest can incorporate activities such as walking, gentle cycling, swimming, using a cross-trainer and very gently running (no more than 20–30 minutes). How well you recover is also dependent on two other things. Firstly, how well you prepared for the race and secondly, how well you looked after yourself during and immediately after the race (hydration, nutrition, sleep, no non-steroidal anti-inflammatories, but turmeric is OK).

The management is to cut back the training and racing until things start improving and then build back up again slowly. This may take several months. The quicker you spot the warning signs and act, the quicker the recovery.

Symptoms of iron deficiency can be very similar, so if the fatigue and poor performance are persistent, see your GP and get some basic blood tests done to ensure that there are no other medical explanations. Be aware that many GPs will have little/no knowledge of overtraining syndrome and chronic fatigue, so you may need to explain to them what is needed. I normally recommend a full (complete) blood count, ferritin, vitamin D, vitamin B12 and folate, renal and liver function, calcium, glucose and thyroid function. If iron deficiency is identified and is persistent then coeliac disease should be excluded with a blood test. This screen covers all the main medical causes for persistent fatigue.

Another cause of poor performance is RED-S – relative energy deficiency in sport. The symptoms overlap with the overtraining syndrome (*see* section on RED-S in Chapter 6).

If there are no identifiable medical causes and the poor performance is persistent, it may be worth getting your training plan reviewed by an experienced coach. The athlete's perception of what constitutes a reduction in training to achieve recovery can be wildly different from mine as their medical adviser. A short period of reduction now is better than struggling on and then needing a longer period of reduction later.

One of the most important lessons of years of running is that less training may actually be better than more. When you see the training plans of the most successful Kenyan distance runners, they are not doing a lot of high-intensity training. This has been formalised in the 80/20 programme, where 80 per cent of training is at low intensity and only 20 per cent at high intensity (*see* Matt Fitzgerald's book in Further Reading). This may not work as well for runners who want to concentrate on short distances. It is particularly important for senior runners to adjust their training, as the older body requires longer recovery periods, so four sessions per week may be better than six or seven.

DEALING WITH INJURY

Injury is an occupational hazard for runners, due to external events (slips, trips, falls) or

'A short period of reduction now is better than struggling on and then needing a longer period of reduction later'

specific training-related injuries. Injuries are covered in more detail in Chapter 9. For specific training or racing-related injury that is not related to external events, it is important to review training and ask the question whether it was preventable. Were you pushing too hard to keep up in a group session? Have you injured a muscle in intervals training? There is a fine line between pushing yourself to improve and pushing yourself to injury. Learning to listen to your body is crucial. If you aren't sure, backing off the training for a few days to assess things is wise and won't dramatically alter your fitness level. A rest may be what you need and may prevent matters progressing to a level where running has to stop completely.

If the injury is a repeat of previous injuries, you need to start asking questions about running style (biomechanics), shoes and unaddressed weaknesses. It can be difficult to disentangle these, and often the quickest route to improvement is to involve a professional. Be aware however that everyone has their own views about how and why things work, which are not always supported by the science, and the science itself changes over time.

It is important to recognise that injury requires rest as the body heals at a fixed rate and frequently runners try to return to running too soon. Being patient and not rushing a return to running is crucial. You may be able to undertake other activities such as swimming, cycling and modified circuit training to help maintain fitness. It is known that, for example, exercising a good leg, while a bad leg is kept immobile, helps preserve muscle function in the injured leg even though it is not exercising.

All runners worry that if they stop running, they will lose fitness. There is no evidence that significant fitness will be lost during a break of up to five days. Beyond five days up to three to four weeks there will be a gradual reduction in fitness, with a decrease in VO_2 max, reductions in cardiac output and decline in the efficiency of metabolism. However, fitness rapidly returns once you start running/exercising again. It is important that you build up again gradually. Beyond one month, fitness declines more significantly and by six months, fitness will have returned entirely to baseline. If you are able, you can maintain a level of fitness by cross-training. Even active walking will help maintain function. It is important to try to maintain a regular routine of alternative activity, as this will help maintain motivation.

Maintaining motivation during periods of injury can be difficult, particularly if key events/goals on your calendar are missed. If you are not fully fit, be careful about doing the event anyway – this is a quick route to a 'DNF' – did not finish. Obviously if you are raising money for charity, it can be more difficult to back out. If you do go ahead, be prepared to be sensible and use a walk-run technique. Most events will have a policy for refunds or transfers.

7 | PREPARING FOR A RACE

Select the events you want to enter carefully. Remember that the longer the event, the longer recovery time you will need to factor in. While it is possible to do superhuman efforts of endurance such as run marathons every day for a month, most of us won't survive that and those who do often pay a significant price down the line. Aim for one or two major events per year and plan the rest of the year in training-and-event terms around these.

If you have decided to enter a race, make sure you allow sufficient time to train properly: be aware that time has a habit of rushing onwards faster than you think. This is where having a proper long-term training plan is important. If the major event is a big one, you may want to enter some shorter races beforehand to use as markers of how training is progressing. Entering major events at the last minute is unwise unless you know you have done the required training.

While it is easy to find published training plans for every conceivable event, remember that the final plan must be tailored to you and may need to be adapted, for example to fit into your existing schedule. If you 'own the plan' you are more likely to stick with it. Plans should always be flexible: you can add more or take a break as you choose. Training

for an event needs to include pushing yourself beyond your comfort zone; further or faster or by including other activities (HIIT circuit, hills). If you stick in your comfort zone your body will never be under any pressure to adapt. The other major reason for pushing yourself is to prevent boredom setting in, which will be the biggest enemy of progression. Try different run routes, alternating short, fast runs with longer, slower runs. Learn to run without being a slave to the watch.

It is worth setting yourself a target for your major event, but this needs to be realistic and achievable. Entering shorter races will give you an idea of sensible and achievable finish times in a longer race. There are lots of online pace calculators (*see* Resources). By working out what pace you need to achieve a particular target time of a given distance, you can practise in training to see whether this is realistic.

Planning needs to be holistic and include all aspects of your life. We recognise the important physical and mental health benefits from running, so it makes sense if life is difficult to make sure that you protect the running time and keep your training going. Training also includes addressing your diet and making sure that you eat enough for the volume of training.

You will undoubtedly have periods when the training is hard, and you feel like giving up. This is where having training partners and supportive family can be a huge help. Also consider online support groups. Cutting down (but not stopping) training for a week can also help you recover. Above all, make sure that you enjoy your training (and your races). While runners love to race, don't forget that getting out and running with no particular goals is equally beneficial, especially for the mind.

When you have specific races in mind, make sure your preparation and training include all aspects of running that you will encounter (off-road, night running, heat, cold, wet, navigation and so on). Practise key skills (*see* Chapter 4) and ensure that you know how you will feed and water yourself before, during and after a race.

TAPERING

While doing the organisational preparation, you also need to consider tapering your training before the event. Tapering allows repair of training-induced muscle damage, and

> '*While runners love to race, don't forget that getting out and running with no particular goals is equally beneficial, especially for the mind*'

the benefit is confirmed in studies that show reduction in blood markers of inflammation and muscle damage. It allows the muscles and liver to maximise glycogen storage. If you are going to taper, this should be from one to two weeks of higher intensity training before the start of the taper and not a gradual run-down of activity over weeks.

Most recreational runners who are not doing high weekly mileage will not need to do much of a taper. If you are one of these, you may wish to reduce your running in the three days prior to the race. Doing absolutely nothing isn't helpful however, as a little bit of running will make the muscles 'hungry' and will maximise the storage of glycogen. A rest the day before the event may be wise.

Higher-performance runners do need to consider tapering. Over how long you do this is going to depend on how long the race is. If it is a really long race, the taper should be longer. At the very least cut down your training to short, easy runs for a few days before the event. Resting completely the day before is a matter of choice. You will not suddenly lose fitness for a few days of reduced activity, provided that your training has gone well. If you are doing a race as part of your training programme for a longer event, a taper may not be necessary – view it as just a faster training run.

Older runners may need to have more of a taper than younger runners, simply to allow the muscles to rest and repair, a process that is slower as you get older.

Part of the taper should include ensuring that your nutrition is appropriate, and this may mean increasing the carbohydrate intake over the days preceding the event. Ensure that your glycogen stores are optimal. Remember that resynthesis of glycogen is maximal after exercise, which is why some exercise in the days before a race is helpful, provided that the exercise is followed by food with carbohydrate.

Try to ensure that you have adequate sleep immediately before races. Performance is impaired by disturbed sleep.

ORGANISATION

Careful planning reduces the stress, but some people are more laid-back in their approach. Whatever works for you. However, I would give some general advice about preparing for events.

1. Entering events

As discussed in the section on training, having a plan for the year enables you to train appropriately. This will include identifying key races. You may have a major target event (first half-marathon or marathon for example) and some subsidiary events that you are using as part of your preparation. Plotting these out at suitable intervals is part of developing the training programme. Some people just like to do events every week for the social element and for fun. Either way, you need to identify appropriate events.

Many popular events are heavily over-subscribed, and some have entry ballots, so there is no guarantee of entry. For major events such as big city marathons and half-marathons, running clubs may have an allocation of places. The other route of entry is via charity places, but this will usually commit you to raising a minimum amount for the charity. For other events be prepared to sit at your computer for a long time on the day entries open to set up an entry (or choose a less popular event!).

Some event organisers offer early-bird entry discounts, but here you are entering races six months or more ahead of time. Discounts can be significant. The risk here is that you may be injured, unwell or other life events may prevent you participating, so check the terms and conditions. It is possible to purchase insurance that covers fees if you cancel. Discounts may also be available if you book a series of events from the same organiser.

If you are planning to do a major challenge, entering early means that the target is fixed and makes it harder to back out. Make sure that you give yourself enough time to train. Most big city events open registrations quite early, often within a month of the previous event finishing.

Many events have a discount for members of officially registered running clubs. You will need to have your England Athletics (or equivalent) registration number to access this. Normally EA registration is done when you join/renew your running club membership. If you don't belong to a running club, you can still get the benefits by joining an online (virtual) running club. For example, Run Things, Lonely Goat and Run Nation (*see* Resources).

Check whether the start will be small-group staggered starts or a mass start, or a choice. You may be given the opportunity to choose a timed start, and it may not be possible to change this later. You may be required to give an estimate of your finishing time. Be realistic about this; if you don't know, make a guesstimate from the time taken for distances in your training. For mass participation events your start position will be allocated according to estimated finish time. Your time won't begin until you cross the timing mat at the start but it may take up to twenty minutes after the gun goes for you to shuffle over the start line. Do not be tempted to put in a ridiculously fast time – it is not fair on other competitors, as you will be slower than them and get in their way.

Make sure you keep your entry confirmation, which may have a registration number on it. The organisers will require this in the event of any queries. The website will show when and how the final race details and race numbers will be sent out/collected.

Check to see whether there are any other special requirements such as photo-ID and make sure you deal with these in time for race day.

2. Travel and accommodation

If the event is a distance away, decide early on how you are going to travel and whether you will need to book accommodation – and think about how you will get your pre-race breakfast, if the start is early. You will need to plan your

> *'Check to see whether there are any other special requirements such as photo ID and make sure you deal with these in time for race day'*

travel to the event to allow time for registration and any unforeseen problems.

3. Race details
Organisers usually make details available two to three weeks ahead of time. Download a copy and either print it off or keep it on your phone. Make sure you have read the instructions carefully. If there are multiple events on the same day, be sure you know what time your event starts. Check the entry list if provided to make sure you're there and if not, contact the organiser.

Check the timings for registration. Most events do not send out race numbers but require you to collect these on the day from the event tent. Parking for some events may be a reasonable walk from the event registration/start, so check this too and plan accordingly.

Check whether there are any special requirements for registration. For many long-distance races off-road, you may be required to present photo ID at registration, as swapping numbers is absolutely prohibited for such events. In some cases, no photo ID means you will not be allowed to run. For some long trail races, registration may open the day before, particularly if there is a very early start. You will not be allowed into the start pen until just before your start time.

For trail races check whether there are any requirements for mandatory kit. Some off-road events will have mandatory kit inspections at registration, and you will not be issued with your race number unless you have the right kit. Organisers may make random spot checks to ensure that after registration you didn't just go back to the car and dump it all. Failure at a spot check will mean disqualification and withdrawal from the race. You have been warned.

It is also worth noting whether there is a facility for drop bags at the finish, into which you can put clothing you have been wearing at the start to keep warm and which you can put on as soon as the race finishes. Check what on-course refreshment stops will be available if any, and what will be offered – you can then tailor what you carry accordingly. Be aware that if you are a slower runner, the faster runners sometimes strip the aid stations of food and drink.

4. One to two days before
Start collecting everything you will need and check through the race details to make sure you have all the required mandatory kit if this is specified. It may be helpful to keep a list of things to take.

Check the weather forecast for the race location, so that you can take appropriate clothing and protection. Make sure you have the shoes in which you plan to race. Check that they are in good condition, and perhaps take a spare pair. Equally if you are unsure of the nature of the terrain for trail races, taking different types of shoes may be wise. Ask at registration what the condition of the course is or chat to other runners who have done it before. On very long races you may have the facility for drop bags, into which you can place clean, dry socks, shoes, spare clothing and food, rather than carry it with you. Make sure these have your name and race number securely attached. These will be transported by the organiser to a pre-determined aid station.

KIT LIST

Your kit list may look like this (not everything is required for every race – for some short road races your kit list may be minimal):

- Running shoes – appropriate for terrain and weather
- Fresh shoes to wear after the event
- Running top (vest, T-shirt, long sleeved)
- Thermal mid layer if appropriate (and in cold weather a spare to go in your race pack)
- Shorts/tights as per weather
- Socks (plus a pair to change into afterwards if you get wet feet)
- Waterproof/windproof jacket and overtrousers according to the weather
- Cap/beanie/Buff/gloves according to weather
- Warm clothing to wear before the start and after the finish
- Anti-chafe cream (I use Vaseline)
- Plasters and/or blister plasters (although if you have tested your kit properly beforehand you should be fine)
- Sunscreen (SPF 30 and above)
- Sunglasses
- Race pack or waist pack with dry bags (or plastic bags with sealers)
- Hydration – flasks, bottles, reservoir bladders and appropriate contents. Check the weather to see how much you are likely to need
- Reusable cup (for races where plastic waste is being reduced)
- Food for on the run (such as gels, energy bars, jelly babies)
- Mandatory kit (check the required list carefully and take spare kit in case the organisers make last-minute alterations)
- Whistle (may be part of your race pack) and torch (for long day races that might go into the night)
- Head torch and spare/spare battery for night races
- Safety pins (don't assume that these will be available at registration, although they usually are) or magnetic number holders for pinning on your race number
- Spare loo roll (there is never enough at races)
- Sports watch and charger
- Mobile phone and charger
- Keys
- Copy of race information and race registration. This may include maps
- Compass and maps if doing an event where navigation is involved and GPS devices are not permitted
- Any travel tickets
- Photo ID (required for many long races)
- If staying away, overnight bag
- Bin bags (useful as cheap weather protection at the start and for putting dirty clothing and shoes in after)

> *'Remember the 5 Ps: Perfect planning prevents poor performance'*

It is better to take more than get to the race and find you don't have something. Weather forecasts have been known to be wrong, so be prepared for anything. If you don't need it, don't take it on the run but if it is 200 miles away at home it is no use. Some races will have stalls from local running stores but not always. If driving, allow plenty of time. The better you plan, the less stress there will be.

MENTAL PREPARATION

I have discussed the importance of mental training in Chapter 6. Preparing mentally for a big race is critical to performance. This means getting into a positive frame of mind: 'I have prepared for this, my training is good, I can do it, I shall enjoy it'. The best way of being in the best frame of mind is planning as above and avoiding unforeseen stress immediately before. If you can offload tasks to trusted family and friends, all the better. Most ultra runners, especially those going for multi-day events, will assemble a team of helpers with a single lead to organise everything. All the runner has to do then is run and not worry about anything else.

Most people will have some degree of anxiety, particularly if it is a big challenge. Some anxiety and the extra adrenaline are helpful and improve performance, but too much will exhaust you. Mindfulness techniques can help. Get to the event in good time, get a feel for it, deal with registration and prepare your race pack/bum bag depending on length of race. It is important to stay warm and keep dry till the start. Once you start your warm-up, this will help get you into the zone and ready to run.

KIT PREPARATION

You need to make sure your kit is in optimal condition. What you need to take will depend on the terrain and weather.

Shoes

Check that these are in good condition, especially where the sole is attached to the upper. They should be clean and dry; get into the habit of cleaning and airing them after events. I use spray-on footwear waterproofer on my trail shoes. Gore-Tex shoes are not great as the water that gets in can't get out. Check the laces. If you are not sure about the terrain, take a choice of shoes and check with organisers/experienced runners on arrival before making a decision.

Clothing

Choose clothing that you know is going to be comfortable and not rub; it is unwise to use brand-new clothing for the first time in a race, and this includes socks. Choose socks that have been used a few times only and have not lost their padding. In winter make sure you have appropriate headwear and gloves. It is worth taking different sorts of clothing in case the weather changes.

Waterproofs

Check these for wear. Check that the waterproof membrane is intact and the taped

This shows the kit to take if you are running in mountains or remote areas. It includes waterproof jacket and overtrousers (an extra long-sleeved top if it's cold). First-aid kit, blister plasters, whistle, compass, torch, map, thermal blanket and bivvy bag, mobile phone, dry bags for phone and clothing and emergency water and food. This will be mandatory kit for mountain races. Add a spare head torch if running at night.

seams have not come away. You can get sealing tape online to reseal seams, but if the inner membrane is fraying the coat will not be waterproof. If there are holes or tears you can buy Gore-Tex patches. Washing waterproof clothing at regular intervals using either Nikwax wash and proofer or Grangers 2-in-1 helps keep the outer surface water repellent (not necessary for jackets that are essentially naked membranes or have a durable water-resistant finish that is bonded to the outer layer).

Race pack/waist pack

Make sure that this is comfortable and will hold what you need to carry for the event. Check straps and fastenings. Like everything else, do not try a new race pack in a race. If the weather forecast indicates rain, make sure you have appropriate dry bags to store key equipment.

Torches

Check that head torches are fully charged. Make sure you have back-up batteries and/or a spare fully charged head torch.

Sports watch

Make sure that this is fully charged and has a big enough battery to last the duration of the event. If it has a battery-saving mode, check the instructions so you know how to activate it. If you have a GPX file of the route, get this uploaded and check you can access this when you need it.

Mobile phone

Make sure that this is fully charged before the race and if you know you will be out for a long time, think about whether a back-up battery may be needed.

8 | RACE DAY AND AFTER

Choose your food carefully the night before. Try to avoid a huge intake of high fibre food and have plenty of carbohydrate. Choose a simple breakfast on the morning of the event. Easily digestible complex carbohydrate is good: porridge is recommended, cereal, toast with butter/peanut butter are all good. If you want the full English, make sure you have tested this out before race day. If possible allow two hours minimum from breakfast to starting gun.

Once you have arrived, head to registration and collect your number +/- timing chip. There may be a large-scale route plan – check this out. Once registered, pin on your number. Some races have specific requirements about where this should be.

In bad weather, do not fasten your number with safety pins through your expensive waterproof jacket as this will leave holes that make the jacket leak: put your number on the running top underneath, but remember to open the jacket as you go through the start and the finish, as the timing chip on the back of the number may not be picked up. At the finish, there may be manual or camera monitoring as a back-up and having a visible number is essential. The same applies if there are intermediate timing mats out on the course to prevent people taking shortcuts.

Check out exactly where the start is. There may be a pre-race briefing. Make sure you arrive in good time to register, get ready and get to the start. Nothing annoys organised runners who are waiting at the start more than being told that there is a delay because of late arrivals!

When you arrive, recheck the weather forecast for the location and adjust your plans for clothing accordingly. Ideally have a thin layer to keep the wind off at the start that can easily be taken off and scrunched down into a waist pack or given to friends/family. If it's sunny, consider using sweatproof suntan cream. If the race is long you may need to take a small tube with you and re-apply from time to time.

Once you have been to registration and collected your number/chip timing device, hopefully you will now have some time to chill out, have a drink (coffee with milk is good) and something light to eat, containing carbohydrate. Allow a minimum of an hour between eating and drinking and the start for digestion to take place.

Consider your feet. If it is going to be wet underfoot, using Vaseline on the skin of the feet stops them getting quite so macerated and blistered. If there are areas on toes or elsewhere that are prone to rubs, tape them or put plasters on beforehand (do this before putting Vaseline on).

In good time, get together any gear you are carrying in the race, hydration and nutrition, get into your race clothing and put on the shoes you will be running in. Consider whether you need to leave anything in the drop bag zone (make sure it has your name and race number on it). Put on any anti-chafe cream on the relevant parts of your anatomy. Make your way to the start. Make sure you put away anything that you take off – don't leave it to the organisers! Aim to do your warm-up somewhere close to the start.

If you have travelled some distance to the event, set up your sports watch well in advance, as it may take it longer to lock on to the GPS signals if you have moved from your usual running location. Don't worry if it turns itself off, it will reload more quickly.

Try to have a plan for the race, based on your training. Have an idea of a target time and an idea of your pace. Checking out the route on a map may give you hints. Are there any long climbing sections or long downhill sections? What is the terrain going to be like? Where are the aid stations and do you know what will be available? Do not be rigid: the best plans are adaptable.

A word of warning: it is most unwise to take anti-inflammatory drugs such as aspirin, ibuprofen and similar before or during a race. These can increase the risk of bleeding if there is an injury and can cause severe kidney problems if you get dehydrated. The Ultra-Trail du Mont Blanc (UTMB) organisers have now banned the use of these drugs before and during their races, and although this has been controversial with runners, it makes sound medical sense. If you must take anything, stick to paracetamol.

WARM-UP

How much of a warm-up you need is a matter of preference. It depends to a large extent on the duration of the race. For very long races (ultra), the first mile or so will be the warm-up and often the start is at walking pace or barely above that. A simple and short (five-minute) dynamic warm-up is useful. This is mainly to get the pulse rate up a little and start increasing the blood flow to muscles. The longer the race, the less you need to warm up. The warm-up also serves to get you mentally into the right frame of mind to perform. Some big races have organised warm-ups with music to get runners into the mood.

Do not stray too far from the start line while warming up and listen for calls to assemble. Depending on the race this may be quite well in advance. For the Great North Run, you are expected to be in your allocated pen 20–30 minutes before the start. Get into your chosen position in the mass start or wait for your timed slot for a staggered start. If the weather is very cold, keep extra layers on for as long

> ### 'If there is a safety briefing, pay attention – it is for your benefit'

PRE-RACE WARM-UP
• Arm swings (mimicking breaststroke is good)
• Upper body twists
• Hip flexions (bend at the hips to touch your toes)
• Squats
• Forward or reverse lunges
• High-knee running on the spot
• Heel kicks to the bottom on the spot
• Alternating side steps
• Massage any sore or tight spots

as possible. When you have stripped down to your race attire, make sure you keep warm: very gentle on-the-spot jogging in position in the mass start (choose a position in the middle, so you are sheltered from wind and rain).

RACE TACTICS AND PSYCHOLOGY

Get your watch ready to press as you pass through the start or over the timing mat. Choose a spot in the mass start appropriate to your estimated time of finishing. Nothing annoys fast runners more than having to dodge round slow runners off the start line.

Check as you pass the start to make sure the button has started the watch. Be wary when taking off clothes during a race to stow in back packs that you do not accidentally press stop on your watch. Some watches have a lock function but if you use this, make sure you know how to stop it as you cross the line.

Beware of going off too quickly. This can be a recipe for disaster later in the race. Try to get into your normal running pattern at a sensible pace. If the race has a steep hill just after the start, be very careful as your muscles may well not be warm enough to do an immediate hill climb – power-walk it. In many mass participation events you won't be able to do anything other than have a slow start because of the crush of people.

You should have an idea from your training what pace you can manage over the distance. There are online calculators which will tell you what pace you have to be running to achieve target times over all the main race distances (*see* Resources). Make sure your targets are realistic and achievable and be prepared to adjust if things are going well or badly.

The use of walk-run techniques can be advantageous. Certainly, on trail runs, it is more efficient to walk the uphill sections, using poles if possible, and run the downhill and flat sections. Some people are frightened that if they stop running and walk, they will not be able to start running again. Make sure you practise the discipline of walking and running in training so it is natural, and be strict; studies have shown that run-walkers are only 3 per cent slower in a marathon than those who run all the way.

Use your watch sensibly to monitor your pace, not too fast nor too slow unless the terrain is harder than expected. Most importantly, listen to your body and be prepared to adjust your race plan as you go. Just as some days in training are simply not good, it will be the same in some races. Go with the flow, slow down and make sure you enjoy it. Use the mental techniques you have developed in training: positive thinking, mantras, self-talk to maintain motivation. Setting yourself in-race targets such as catching the next runner ahead are helpful. Try to get an even pace throughout the race, or better try for a negative split, that is doing the second half slightly quicker. It is better to do the first half slightly more slowly and then pick up the pace for the second half, rather than going off too fast and slowing up in the second half and struggling to finish. Always save a little bit for the final kick-on in the last half to one mile. You want to cross the finish line going quickly with good running form to impress friends and family!

As you tire, you will tense up. Stride length will shorten (marathon shuffle). Learn to recognise this and deal with it. The tension increases tiredness. Practise relaxing the upper body, use visualisation, focus on the surroundings, watch other runners, look at their gait. Adjust your stride and body posture. Do some surges or strides. Make sure you keep the upper body straight.

Try to smile. Smiling has been shown to reduce the perceived effort of activities. Smile at spectators, marshals and especially the photographer.

Revise the sections on hydration and nutrition before the race. Use your fluids carefully: small regular sips rather than huge mouthfuls. If it is hot, you will obviously need more. Take on calories at intervals. You probably need a gel sachet an hour of running time: more frequent is likely to upset your stomach. For long races, you should have alternatives to gels, such as energy bars, food sachets or jelly babies. When you get to aid stations take your time to have a drink, eat and top up water bottles. Many races, especially trail races, have stopped providing water in bottles or plastic cups and expect you to bring your own re-usable collapsible cup. Perhaps walk for a short distance to allow the food/fluid to settle.

When you are approaching the finish make sure your number is visible. This ensures that the timing chip (if on the back of the number) will be read, but if it isn't then the race organisers back-up system will pick you up. Timing chips do fail from time to time, so if you don't appear where you expect to on the post-race finish list, contact the organisers and they can manually verify your finish time. Also get ready to stop your own watch as you cross the line.

If everything goes pear-shaped in the race, do not be afraid to drop out. You will do yourself less harm than struggling on and making an injury worse. No one likes a DNF (did not finish), but sometimes it is just the most prudent course of action. Hopefully with careful and appropriate training, your risks of a DNF will be low. If you stop on the course, make sure you inform the organisers either directly or via a marshal (if they have walkie-talkies), especially if it is a trail run, to avoid search parties being sent out to find you. Some races will have a 'sweeper' who will follow round behind the last runner, to ensure that everyone is safe.

> ## 'If everything goes pear-shaped in the race, do not be afraid to drop out'

RACE ETIQUETTE

Behaving well during races is important. Be considerate to fellow runners and to the organising crew. Races are not just about you. Sadly, in the return to racing post-Covid there have been reports from race organisers of unacceptable behaviour. There are some key areas to think about.

Race registration

The volunteers manning registration desks will be dealing with hundreds of competitors. Do them the favour of arriving in good time and be polite. Your race number may have been allocated in advance and can be checked online, so make sure you know it. The start lists may be on a board in the registration tent.

Swapping numbers

If you cannot compete for whatever reason, you should not give your number to anyone without informing the organisers. Many entry forms require you to give basic medical information and if the organisers are unaware of a swap and something happens, inappropriate information may be given to the emergency services. Some over-subscribed events prohibit passing your entry to another person, as they will often have their own waiting lists. They may offer you a refund or the option to defer your entry.

This is particularly important for long-distance races, which may require photographic ID at registration and will have your name on your race number.

The start

Mass starts can be difficult. If you know you are a slower runner, start further back to give the quick runners a clear start. There is plenty of time for the race, so pushing and shoving isn't necessary.

During the race

Be considerate to other competitors, especially on narrow tracks/trails. Call out to say you are passing (and indicate which side) – choose a suitable place to overtake. While draughting (sitting on someone's shoulder to get free drag) is good for you, it is considered bad form, unless you are running with friends and have agreed to take it in turns to lead. Keep running poles out of other people's way. On many trail races, faster runners may set off after you, so you may well be caught by them. It is helpful to call a warning to runners ahead ('fast runner') and to move off the track to let them through and if using poles, keep them out of the way. At refreshment stations, wait your turn patiently. The same at stiles and narrow gates. If you need to slow down or start walking, pull over to one side to allow faster people through. If you are going to do a walking start, start at the back.

Be supportive and encouraging to other runners, particularly if they seem to be struggling. Sometimes slowing down and encouraging another runner is all that is required to get them going again. Be prepared to stop and help any fellow runner in difficulty, and, if necessary, seek assistance either from marshals or via emergency services. Some races will give out a specific emergency number to call. If they do, make sure it is in your phone. Someone must stay with an injured runner until help arrives and they must be kept warm. Remember – this could be you next time, so the dash for a personal best can wait.

Take all your waste away with you: do not drop any rubbish, particularly on trail runs. Aid stations will have bins.

I know that for many, the races are a social occasion, but some people seem able to talk incessantly throughout the whole of a race. This is quite distracting for quieter runners, so be considerate.

Marshals

Events will not take place unless there are adequate marshals. The marshals are volunteers who give up their free time so you can enjoy yours.

Remember this and treat them with respect. Please thank each marshal you pass. This may be self-evident, but you would be surprised how rude some runners are to marshals.

At road crossings, marshals do not have the authority to stop traffic. They must therefore ask you to wait to allow cars to pass and can then indicate that you are free to cross. Follow their instructions. Marshals are also there to remind runners of any specific rules that the organisers have applied to the race – these will be in the race information and/or the pre-race briefing. Failure to comply will be reported to the race organiser.

If you are not able to run, consider volunteering to marshal: organisers always need more.

Spitting

Spitting is most unhygienic and is unnecessary. Covid has reinforced this and many races now have a specific ban. If you think you might need to either spit or clear your nose, take a

> *'The marshals are volunteers who give up their free time so you can enjoy yours'*

handkerchief or get right off the track away from other people.

Cheating

You might think that no one would want to cheat, but you would be wrong! Most big city marathons now have randomly placed timing mats on course and their timing computers will flag unusual times on sections that might suggest someone has taken a shortcut. A runner was caught cheating in the Kielder marathon: he caught a spectator bus for part of the route, re-joined the course just before the finish, and came in third. The person who finished behind him (a policeman!) knew that he had not been in front of him and had not passed him, so registered a complaint. Witnesses had seen him getting on the bus. He was disqualified and banned, which was a pity because he was good enough to have come in the top ten anyway. He was caught the next year entering the Great North Run while still banned, using a friend's name and competed wearing sunglasses. Nonetheless he was recognised. Entering under a false name is against the rules for races – so further bans where imposed.

At the end of the day, if you cheat you are cheating yourself and fellow runners – so don't even think about it.

PROBLEMS IN THE RACE

Even with the best preparation and planning, things may go pear-shaped during the race.

Injuries

These can include trips and falls, twisted ankles, cuts and bruises. If you have a first-aid pack, you can manage minor injuries. More serious injuries require assistance, either by summoning help on the phone or via a marshal.

Blisters/Chafing

Having specific blister plasters with you is helpful. Prevention is better than cure; if kit has been carefully selected for fit and comfort, blisters should be uncommon. However, running for long periods with wet feet increases the risk, hence the suggestion to pre-treat the feet with Vaseline if wet conditions are expected. Likewise chafing can be prevented by using anti-chafing creams or Vaseline.

Cramps

These are usually due to either dehydration or salt depletion or both. They can also occur for example where there are long downhill sections. Stopping and doing stretches will help, as will increasing fluid intake, with electrolytes (preferably a solution that contains some calcium and magnesium as well as salt).

Stomach cramps

These can be brought on by eating/drinking too much in one go: prevention is best by having small amounts continuously through the run. If it becomes a repetitive problem, it is worth reviewing your pre-race diet, and avoiding high-fibre foods. In very long, hard races, the bowel becomes very short of oxygen, as blood is directed away to the muscles and this will cause cramps. Slowing down for a while will help. Sometimes the cramps will be accompanied by an overwhelming desire to empty the bowels. If it happens regularly, you should discuss with your GP whether antispasmodics might be helpful.

Vomiting

Vomiting usually has similar causes to stomach cramps. If you are vomiting a lot, it rapidly becomes hard to maintain hydration. Walking and trying to sip fluids with sugar and electrolytes slowly can help, but if it will not settle then it may be best to withdraw.

Dizziness and Confusion

Dizziness and confusion are serious signs (*see* Chapter 9) but often runners are unaware of the gradual onset. Dizziness can be due to dehydration or low blood sugar. Make sure that you race with a plan for eating and drinking where a race is over an hour. Astute marshals or personnel at aid stations may recognise it and pull people aside, but they cannot force people to stop.

Remember – there is no shame in stopping and pulling out of a race. Experienced runners have all had to do it. It is better to do this than risk further injury or serious illness.

ULTRA AND MOUNTAIN RACES

Racing in mountains needs special care. Make sure you have carefully read and complied with any pre-race instructions from the organisers. Check the mandatory kit list. There is likely to be a published route, unless it is an orienteering event where you are expected to devise your own route to and from a series of fixed points. If there is a GPX file (a list of all the waypoints which navigation devices can overlay onto a map), download it and study it in advance. Check kit very carefully to make sure it is in good condition, especially shoes.

Most ultras and mountain races will have cut-offs for reaching check points. If you exceed the cut-off, you will be timed out and unable to complete the race. Look carefully at the cut-offs and compare these with the terrain you will be crossing. They may appear generous, but if you are doing a lot of climbing on technical terrain (aka rough, rocky, pathless terrain) then your pace will be slow. If you are looking for a first ultra this is very important.

Choose one with generous cut-offs that can be achieved by walking and preferably one without a lot of climbing or technical terrain. On level ground, walking pace should be between 3–4 miles per hour, slowing to around 2 mph uphill. Calculate a realistic minimum and maximum time for the route and check against the cut-offs.

Weather can change very suddenly, so make sure that you have emergency clothing and extra food and drink. For multiday races you may be camping, so you may be carrying a lightweight tent and sleeping bag plus extra food and drink. Be prepared to be walking for chunks, particularly uphill or technical sections. Navigation skills are essential. Organisers may require you to carry a tracking device. Make sure you understand the course and listen to the race briefing and any last-minute instructions.

If there are few/no aid stations, then you will have to carry enough fluid. While you can drink from some streams, there are significant risks of infection; you could carry water disinfection tablets and a filter bottle that can be used to purify water on the run. The tablets may leave the water with a chemical taste but this is better than developing severe gastroenteritis.

Ideally, try to run with a friend or a group, so if there are problems there is someone who can help.

AFTER THE RACE

As you finish, enjoy the moment and try to smile – there will usually be a photographer at the finish for major races. Congratulate yourself, no matter how the race went. After the race, collect your mementos, make sure you eat and drink and have a rest before setting off home.

The body will be avid for sugar to rebuild its glycogen stores. Enjoy the atmosphere. If you can, stay and cheer in slower runners – it makes a difference to them. Race organisers do appreciate thanks, if you get the chance.

Enjoy the moment – a hard-earned medal for a first half-marathon! Reproduced with permission of Anne Harper.

> *'Post-race recovery is extremely important and failure to allow sufficient time for this is a fast-track to overtraining and injury'*

For many events, the organisers will have arranged for a photographer to be present. Photos can be part of the race package and simply downloaded from the internet, or bought from the photographer.

If you have raised money for charity, make sure that it is collected up and handed over promptly. Keep the receipt in case anyone queries where the money has gone (you never know).

POST-RACE RECOVERY

Post-race recovery is extremely important and failure to allow sufficient time for this is a fast-track to overtraining and injury.

How you are post-run/race will depend on how fit and prepared you were before the run, how well you have looked after yourself during the run and how far and how difficult the run has been.

Recovery can be divided into an immediate phase straight after finishing a race, steps to take over the next few days and then the approach to returning to training. This section also applies to recovery after intense, long training sessions.

Immediately after a race

When you have finished the race, you will undoubtedly be elated to have crossed the finish line. Your adrenaline levels will still be high. Preferably have some clean socks and different trainers to change into as your feet will be larger at the end of the run.

If you have any minor injuries and there is an on-site first-aid station, get them seen to. Delay may lead to serious infection. Even a minor graze can lead to devastating infection if not cleaned properly.

The most immediate requirement will be to address your hydration. You may continue to sweat for a while after you stop running, so you will need to continue drinking. Fluid is also required to replace glycogen. This should be a mixture of fluids (electrolyte solutions, water) but avoid dehydrating drinks like tea or coffee. Beer is said to be good as it contains calories, electrolytes and fluid – but use this with caution (and not at all if you are driving)!

Once you have addressed clothing and fluid, the next stage is food. Your body will be desperate to replace energy stores and will avidly take up sugar after exercise. Adding in some fat and protein will be beneficial. If the event has food outlets at the finish, try to use them. If you know that there will be no on-site food outlets, and none nearby, make sure you pack a post-race snack.

If you are driving yourself and it is a fair distance, make sure you have a walk around

KEY FEATURES OF POST-RACE RECOVERY
• Hydration
• Nutrition
• Rest
• Muscle recovery
• Sleep
• Dealing with injury

before setting off. Cramp can be a problem when driving and this will be reduced if you have addressed food and drinks before setting off, so that your concentration is maintained. Remember, your brain needs glucose to function properly and if you have used up your glycogen and not replaced it, your brain will not function, causing disorientation and confusion.

Should I do static stretches?
The jury is out on this. Gentle stretches may certainly help, provided they do not cause pain. If you have a long drive back, stretching before you get into the car is sensible and may prevent cramps.

Should I get a massage?
Bigger races often have physiotherapists at the finish offering massages (usually for a fee). The research doesn't indicate that having a massage helps recovery but there is a strong placebo element. You may feel better, even if the muscles don't recover faster.

Should I have a cold bath/shower or ice bath?
The benefits of ice baths for recovery seem to be indelibly written into post-race mythology. The research has shown that a hot bath or shower may be more effective. Sore muscles need to have a good blood supply and an ice bath will shut down blood supply to limbs. The science shows that cold immersion post-exercise decreases the production of the proteins required for muscle repair, whereas warmth increases the production. Running performance is worse when cold immersion has been used post-run. But if you feel it helps, then the placebo effect will probably mean that you benefit.

Should I use compression garments?
While there is conflicting scientific evidence to support benefit from compression garments during events, there is more agreement that using compression garments post-race is helpful in supporting tired and sore muscles. Part of the problem is that there is wide variability in the level of compression in garments. Compression should be graduated, being higher at the feet/ankles and decreasing up the leg.

Endurance training improves muscle repair
It has been shown that endurance exercise over time improves the ability of muscles to repair themselves. The more training you do (within sensible limits), the better the muscles become at healing themselves and the faster you will recover.

Do supplements help recovery?
This is not so clear cut. There is evidence that fish oil helps recovery and that branch-chain amino acids (BCAA) are required for muscle repair. The latter are usually found in recovery drinks. My personal experience is that BCAAs do reduce the amount of muscle soreness, which suggests that repair is happening quicker. They need to be taken soon after a run/race.

Sleep
When you get home the adrenaline will be wearing off and fatigue will set in. You may paradoxically find it difficult to get to sleep on the first night. Muscles may be achey and you may just be generally restless. Allow adequate time for sleep – it is important.

THE NEXT FEW DAYS

Over the next few days, expect the muscles to become more sore (DOMS = delayed onset muscle soreness), particularly where there has

---

'Allow adequate time for sleep – it is important'

---

been steep downhill running. There is not a great deal that you can do either to prevent or treat it. Gentle exercise (walking) is good, and massage may help. Avoid rushing back to training until it has settled down.

If you have any soft tissue injuries, remember the drill of PRICE: protection, rest, ice, compression and elevation. If an injury does not settle promptly with simple measures, seek further professional advice.

Foam rolling, both with smooth and spiky foam rollers, is frequently recommended. Like massage and many other recovery strategies, the benefit may be more psychological than physiological. There is no evidence for harm, and if you feel it helps then do it.

There is some scientific evidence that having an increased intake of branch-chain amino acids (BCAA) before and after exercise may help, as these are essential for muscle building and repair. Whether you need supplements is debatable, as these amino acids are found in a wide variety of foodstuffs, including a lot of grains and legumes. Buying them as supplements is expensive and having a good broadly based diet may well be just as effective. Milk is a very effective recovery food that contains pretty much everything you need, including BCAA.

Other supplements have been studied and of these, cherry juice appears to be the most promising, with studies showing that it accelerates recovery and improves muscle function. Curcumin (the active ingredient of turmeric) has also been shown to be beneficial, both for reducing muscle damage during exercise and improving recovery after. Both cherry juice and curcumin are powerful antioxidants and anti-inflammatories.

Sleep is important: try to get as much as you can. Sleep is linked to the body's hormonal profiles and this in turn is linked to recovery and muscular repair.

Reduced immunity to infections is common for up to 72 hours after a hard race. Obviously at a big race the chances of transmission of respiratory infections are high. While not exactly preventable, a good diet and plenty of vitamin C can help reduce the chances of picking something up.

A lot of the post-activity recovery studies have all come to the same conclusions that there is often little actual supporting science, but that athletes' beliefs that certain activities are helpful have a placebo effect. This is still a good reason to undertake the activities.

RETURN TO TRAINING

After a big race, you should not be in a hurry to return to training. Allow two to three days of minimal activity (just walking) before you start running gently. If the race was your major event of the year, allow yourself a break for a week or two – you will not lose significant fitness in this time and it allows your body to recover fully. A rule of thumb is one day of rest for every hour of the race. As part of the periodisation, ease back in with shorter gentle runs to begin with (20–30 minutes) and use other activities such as walking, yoga, cycling, swimming or cross-trainers. If things have gone well, you may get too ambitious in terms of entering more events and risk burning yourself out.

If there are any persisting niggles or injuries, make sure that these are addressed promptly.

Take the time to assess how the race went: did it go as expected, better or worse? Is there anything that you could have done differently in the run-up to the race that would have improved the outcome? Was the training right and does it need to be changed? Use your training log to record your thoughts and amend your next block of training.

After a major race you will need to address your motivation. You will have invested a lot in the preparation and when the immediate elation wears off, you can be left feeling very flat. This is where having a training group or

> *'This is where having long-term goals and not just short-term goals is really important'*

a running club can be most helpful – as well as giving you the opportunity to humble-brag by wearing your event T-shirt! Be positive and think about what comes next; a longer race, a different race? Start planning. This is where having long-term goals and not just short-term goals is really important.

Review performance

After each race, you should review your performance, with how you felt and the data your watch has recorded. Keep a record of key data, so that you can go back and compare. Think about what went well and what went badly, what lessons you learned and how you can improve weaknesses. You need to incorporate these thoughts into your next training programme. Be careful, as the excitement of a really good finish can lead to the basic error of overtraining. If you have a coach or training group, it is helpful to run your thoughts past them for validation or comment.

If you have 'unexplained under-performance syndrome' (UUPS), then you need to look very carefully at all factors in your training and preparation and analyse how you ran the race. Some factors may be easier than others to deal with, for example going off too fast at the start and running out of steam. Failing to get fuelling and hydration right throughout the race is another easily remediable cause.

You can get caught out on race day by weather changes.

Think not only about the actual race stats, but also consider all aspects of the preparation. You may want to do the race again next year. Was the travel/accommodation satisfactory? Did you get to the event at the right time? Use your training log to record important information for next time.

Equally you will want to decide whether you really enjoyed race day. This is more than just the course itself, but the overall organisation. Is it one that you would recommend to a friend and want to go back and do again? On the whole organisers are keen to have runners' feedback, so they can improve the event for subsequent years, but they do get fed up with social media criticism. Why not think about volunteering to help?

Dealing with a DNF

A 'did not finish' (DNF) is always a serious disappointment. You should always try to take positives away even from the most negative event. What was the reason: illness, injury or weather for example? As with any race, you still need to do a realistic assessment of what went wrong and what went well. Always look for the positives: 'I was running strongly until I tripped and turned my ankle'; 'I coped better than usual with the uphill section'.

The most important thing about a DNF is to pick yourself up, sort out illness/injury and get back to training with a positive frame of mind. You may already have another event booked. Consider realistically whether you can do it. If the answer is no, withdraw in good time. The need to prove yourself to yourself may make you rush recovery and do too much too soon. This will just make the whole process of recovery take longer. Re-evaluate your training and add in the necessary elements to improve performance.

Example: You had a DNF in a trail race because you fell on a downhill section, twisted your ankle and cut your hand.

Using root cause analysis, you would look at all the possibilities:

- Was my downhill running technique good?
- Were my legs sore?
- Was I too tired?
- Did I lose concentration (talking to a fellow runner)?
- Was the track slippery?
- Did I have appropriate grippy shoes?
- Was I using poles to balance and if so, was I using them correctly?
- Had I trained on similar terrain/ conditions?

For all of these, you need to investigate further and then conclude what the major and contributory factors were and seek to address them in better training and equipment planning.

Using the 5 Whys:
- I fell on a rock downhill section – why?
- My legs were hurting – why?
- Not used to running downhill and slipped – why?
- Poor running form and wrong shoes – why?
- Poor training and shoe selection – why?

Conclusion: need to address training and practise on similar terrain; investigate best shoes for this terrain.

You can use analysis techniques such as root cause analysis (RCA) and '5 Whys'. The purpose of this is to get beneath the surface of a problem to understand why it arose in the first place. This sort of analysis will then help you draw important conclusions from your DNF and enable you to do better next time.

Falling out of love with running

Everyone falls out of love with running at some point, especially if a major target has been completed or there has been disappointment. Having a break from running is a good idea but keep fit by doing other activities. The desire to run will return!

9 | INJURIES AND ILLNESS

While some degree of self-diagnosis and self-help is appropriate, any severe or persistent injury or illness is an indication to seek professional help promptly. Early diagnosis and treatment will often lead to a more rapid return to training.

For musculoskeletal problems, the best starting point is a specialist sports physiotherapist. For persistent or recurrent running injuries, assessment by a running coach familiar with gait analysis may be appropriate. For illnesses, the first port of call will be your GP.

COMMON RUNNING INJURIES

Acute injuries should be treated with PRICE (protection, rest, ice, compression and elevation) as first aid. The role of ice and compression is to reduce acute swelling which can sometimes be more dangerous than the original injury. Any acute and significant injury should be evaluated in A&E, or if less acute or persistent by a qualified sports physiotherapist. Most large running events will have a first-aid tent staffed by paramedics who can give immediate care and advise about follow-up care.

If you are injured, you need to be patient. You can usually maintain fitness in other non-running activities unless the injury is a major one. Other activities such as swimming or aqua jogging can be helpful. Obviously cross-training will help maintain cardiovascular fitness but not specifically help with running fitness. The return to running needs to be slow and controlled, starting, if necessary, with walking and then building up to walk-run. If the pain returns, stop or reduce activity. Do not force yourself to run differently, that is do not run limping or favouring the good leg: all that this achieves is creating a significant risk of a new injury in a different location.

For fit runners, the good news is that muscles retain a 'memory' of their previous trained state, so that muscle recovery after injury is quicker than in people who were not fit before the injury.

A word on taping. You will see lots of runners whose legs are crisscrossed with physio tape (a favourite tool of physiotherapists). There are definite injuries that benefit from this (Achilles tendon, plantar fasciitis, knee pain), but often the tape is being applied in places where the only benefit would be psychological. Like everything in running mythology, as long as it isn't harmful and you think it helps, there is no reason to stop.

Foam rollers are like Marmite; you either love them or hate them. They can be very

- Train and race sensibly, allowing sufficient rest and recovery time
- Incorporate specific strength and conditioning sessions into your programme
- Ensure that clothing and shoes fit properly, are comfortable and are appropriate for the type of running
- Replace worn-out shoes promptly but beware that new shoes, especially of a different type, may trigger injury
- If you are tired or unwell do not run, or reduce the distance/pace
- Do not get forced into activities by friends or running groups that you do not feel comfortable with
- Check weather conditions before runs, especially in cold weather when there may be ice
- Concentrate when running off-road to avoid trip/fall hazards
- Use a walk-run technique on long runs
- Avoid running continuously on a sloping surface (such as heavily cambered road or beach)
- Use appropriate and correct stretching after exercise
- Do not run when injured
- Warm up and cool down properly, especially if doing speedwork
- Do not ignore minor niggles. Treat as appropriate and modify training, if necessary, to prevent a minor niggle turning into a major problem
- Men and women are prone to different injuries due to the different biomechanics – gait analysis can help
- Increase mileage gradually, not suddenly
- Introduce uphill and downhill running (both on and off-road) gradually
- Introduce speedwork carefully, especially if you are an older runner
- Be very careful about introducing plyometrics (jump-based) exercises: start with low heights first and build up gradually

useful for helping to release tight muscles or deal with painful spots. Hockey balls are useful for rolling small, localised areas of painful muscles, especially feet. Percussion massagers can be very useful for dealing with tight or painful spots in muscles. The best known and most expensive is Theragun, but there are plenty of alternatives available.

This book is not a comprehensive account of all possible injuries and is not a substitute for getting proper professional advice. A very good resource, covering most common injuries is Metzl and Zimmerman's book, *The Athlete's Book of Home Remedies* (*see* Resources). This covers all major injuries, explains the anatomy, causes and treatment. As Dr Metzl is a medically

qualified runner, this is a reliable guide. For more detailed information see *Running Injuries* by Galloway and Hannaford (*see* Resources), but again the bottom line is for significant injuries or injuries that do not improve with rest, professional advice early is required.

Toenails

Black toenails and/or loss of toenails is a very common problem in runners (*see* Chapter 3). On trails, impact of the toes on rocks can cause bruising/bleeding under the toenail which can be very painful. Fungal nail and skin infections are common especially if the feet get wet or very sweaty. Wash and dry feet promptly and use anti-fungal treatments if necessary.

Blisters and calluses

Blisters occur at sites of prolonged pressure or abrasion. They are more likely to occur when the skin is soft and wet. Any anatomical abnormality, for example bunions, will increase the risk. Keys to prevention include making sure that shoes do not rub. Shoes should be of a size that will accommodate the swelling of the feet during a run, but not so large that the foot slides around in the shoe. Double-layer socks may help, as the layers of the sock slip against each other and not the skin. Choose socks that have high wicking properties (not cotton, which will just soak up the sweat). Merino wool-based socks and Coolmax are excellent. Taping areas of the foot that are prone to blisters is helpful when done as a preventive measure. Using pressure padding (Moleskin Plus from Dr Scholl or generic equivalents) is also an option. With some shoes, more space can be created in the toe box by omitting the first set of eyelets for lacing.

There is always debate about whether blisters should be drained. Small blisters can be left to resolve, with appropriate padding over them to prevent further damage. Large blisters are best drained, using a sterile process, as the blister fluid is highly inflammatory and will cause continuing pain. Clean the area with an antiseptic wipe and then pierce the blister at the lowest point, furthest away from the body, so that it drains effectively, then cover with a sterile dressing taped very firmly down. Do not remove the roof of the blister as this will protect the underlying tissues and may re-attach. This is best done by the first-aid teams at long events. After events, blisters should be protected and kept as clean, dry and well aired as possible. Use a blister specific plaster if possible and change it if it gets wet. Seek prompt medical assistance if there are signs of infection.

If you have medical conditions that reduce the sensation in the feet, for example any type of sensory neuropathy, including complications of diabetes, then it is especially important to take great care.

Calluses can form at sites of long-term friction and may become painful. Excess skin can be sanded away, but small calluses have a protective function. They are however an indicator to check footwear to identify why the excess friction is occurring.

Cuts, grazes and puncture wounds

Bleeding should be stopped with pressure. Wounds need to be promptly cleaned with a soap/disinfectant combination and any foreign material removed to prevent infection. Even minor cuts and grazes should be cleaned promptly as they can still cause serious local infection. Large, dirty wounds may best be treated in a walk-in centre; a tetanus booster may be required. Large or deep cuts may need stitching. Steristrips can be used temporarily, but deep wounds should not be closed with stitches or steristrips until they have been properly cleaned and inspected. Profuse venous or arterial bleeding can be life threatening. Apply firm pressure and seek immediate help.

> *'Profuse venous or arterial bleeding can be life threatening. Apply firm pressure and seek immediate help'*

Chafed nipples

Chafed nipples are a relatively common problem in both sexes. Over a long race this can cause significant discomfort and prevention is better than cure. Specific creams, tapes and nipple shields are available (*see* Resources for Health). Wear soft fabrics to reduce rubbing. I use Vaseline and put a strip of micropore tape over the top.

Fractures

Fractures typically occur in the lower leg and ankle, but also hands/wrists/forearm (outstretched hand when falling). Mostly people will be immediately and acutely aware, feeling or hearing the crack. Fractures may be closed or open, where the skin is pierced by the sharp bone ends. Fractures may be accompanied by dislocations, where joints are disrupted. This can be very dangerous around the ankle where the deformity and swelling can damage the blood supply and/or nerves to the foot. First aid includes covering any open wounds, loosening any tight footwear, removing rings/watches where wrists or hands are involved and immobilising the injured limb.

Bites and stings

It is worth using a potent insect repellent. Be aware that some insect repellents will damage plastics, so avoid getting them on your expensive sports watch. Nettles and brambles can also make life unpleasant. If you know you are going to be running on rough terrain with high grass and bracken, wear long tights. Make sure you have your emergency treatment pack with relevant medication if you react badly to stings, and wear a Medic-Alert (or equivalent) bracelet or necklace. Tick bites can transmit a variety of infections including Lyme disease. Ticks should be removed as soon as possible with a tick remover (carry one with you on multi-day events), ensuring that the mouthparts are completely removed. If you feel unwell after a tick bite and/or you develop the typical target lesion, see a doctor at once and explain that you have had a tick bite. Antibiotics will be required.

Snake bites in the UK are rare and will be from adders. You will be more at risk when running on rough terrain without paths. Mostly the adders will sense you coming and move away. Apply a pressure immobilisation bandage and seek immediate help. If you are travelling to more exotic places to run/race, get specific advice on potential hazards such as venomous spiders and snakes.

Side stitch (exercise-related transient abdominal pain: ETAP)

Up to two-thirds of runners will experience a stitch at some point. This is usually stabbing pain just under the ribcage, and occasionally radiating to the tip of the shoulder. The cause is unclear, so prevention and treatment are guesswork. Symptoms will resolve with rest (if they don't then something else is wrong and medical advice should be sought). If you are prone to stitches, don't overeat or drink before setting off; when drinking or eating on the run take small sips or bites; do S&C exercises to improve core muscle strength. To treat a stitch, stop running and walk, press on the affected area and take deep breaths, bend forward and do toe touches.

Metatarsalgia

This is pain across the underside of the front of the foot but not the toes. It can be caused by a change of shoes or by sudden increases in distance, especially in new runners. Shoes that are too tight or lack cushioning under the forefoot will also trigger metatarsalgia. High arched feet are more likely to develop it. Treatment includes cutting back on distance or taking a few days' rest, checking shoes for correct size and considering a more cushioned insole or thicker cushioned socks.

Morton's neuroma

This is a swelling in the nerve, often between the third and fourth toes, which causes pain under or over the affected toes, made worse by walking and running. Wearing shoes that are too small or have inadequate room for the forefoot is often a trigger. The trend now is to have running shoes with much wider toe boxes which should help reduce the risk. Treatment can be difficult and sometimes surgery is necessary. Professional advice is most definitely required.

Stress fractures

Stress fractures can occur at any time and in any bone, although the commonest sites are the metatarsal and shin bones. Pain is the main symptom. Thin bones (osteopenia, osteoporosis) will contribute. Most are caused by excessive mileage or a sudden stress. Diagnosis may be difficult initially as X-rays may not show anything, but if repeated after an interval will show

damage. While it is possible to run through stress fractures, this is unwise as they can convert to a complete fracture. Rest, supportive shoes and patience are required. Most minor ones will resolve over six weeks, although there should be no running for at least eight weeks. Specialist advice is recommended.

Plantar fasciitis

This is a common running problem and causes pain underneath the heel, at the back of the heel and under the arch of the foot. The plantar fascia is a band of tough, fibrous tissue that holds the arch in place linking the toes to the heels. It provides the 'spring' in the foot and acts a bit like the carbon fibre plates in running shoes. It can be caused by running in old and/or poorly supportive shoes and be triggered by jump exercises. Treatment can involve supportive strapping, using physio tape and massage of the underside of the foot with a hard ball. It can be quite persistent, although may not necessarily stop you running altogether.

Ankle injury

The ankle is particularly prone to soft tissue injuries, particularly when it rolls inward or outward too far, damaging the ligaments that hold the joints together (sprains). Fractures can occur if the force is extreme. If symptoms are mild, they may settle with continued walking and gentle running. However, if the pain is severe and/or the ankle swells rapidly, seeking help is neces-

'If you are limping, it is too soon to try running'

sary. Apply RICE (rest, ice, compression and elevation) until evaluated. Minor sprains should settle in three to six weeks. Sprains where the ankle is forced outwards take longer to heal. During recovery, practising balance exercises is helpful. If you are limping, it is too soon to try running. When you do run, any recurrence of severe pain is an indication to stop.

Shin splints

Pains down the front of the shin bone are common in beginners and more experienced runners when the mileage is suddenly increased. It is caused by irritation to fibrous tissue surrounding the bone, especially at sites where muscles are inserted, due to the pulling of the muscles. Hill running and excessive heel-strike are contributory factors. Treatment is ice and massage and reducing mileage, while continuing to run. Reviewing your shoes and getting gait analysis may also be helpful. If the pain doesn't settle or gets worse, professional review is advisable, as similar symptoms can be seen with stress fractures of the shin bones.

Achilles tendon injuries

Achilles tendon injuries are common in runners, as the tendon is the major connection of the calf muscles to the ankle. Pain can be over the tendon, radiate into the heel or up into the back of the calf. Pinching the tendon will invariably be painful and you may be able to see and feel swelling. Sudden onset of severe pain and difficulty walking can indicate a partial or full rupture of the tendon, which is a serious injury that may require surgical repair and is likely to stop you running for a considerable time. This is most likely to be seen when doing sprints. Sudden increases in mileage and uphill and downhill running are contributory factors. If symptoms are mild, you can continue to run. Using an elasti-cated ankle support may help, or using physio tape to support the tendon (apply with ankle extended, toes pointing down).

Patello-femoral knee pain

The kneecap connects the quads to the knee and directs the force of contraction around the knee itself. Pain can occur at the top and the bottom, and the back of the kneecap that faces the knee joint itself can be affected by arthritis. The shape of the various bones and how they join together is a major factor in determining whether knee pain is likely to occur. Downhill running, jump-based exercises and weightlifting are all potential causes. Mild knee pain is not a contraindication to running and will often improve as the muscles strengthen. Doing exercises specifically to strengthen the quads and other muscles around the knee will help significantly. Wearing knee supports may help, although you need to get one that is really supportive and comfortable. Physios sometimes use taping techniques to provide support and reduce abnormal movement. Persistent or worsening pain is of course an indication for professional advice.

ITB problems

The iliotibial band (ITB) is an extremely thick band of tissue connected to the outer part of the hip by muscle fibres at the top and running down the outside of the thigh to the knee. Its purpose is to stabilise the knee during walking and running. If there are problems, the pain is usually felt on the outside of the knee. Similar pain can occur with damage to the outer part of the hamstring muscles. The ITB is not very elastic and although exercises and foam rolling are advised, the evidence for benefit is unclear. Injuries to the ITB often take a considerable time to heal. If symptoms are mild, then there is no contraindication to running but if symptoms worsen then rest is required. Checking gait and shoes is wise.

Hip and gluteal problems

Pain on the inside of the hip is usually due to strains to the muscles that attach to the hip and pelvis on the inside (adductors). This is one of the causes of groin strain beloved of footballers. These muscles are at risk of damage when striding out or during sudden lateral movements. This sort of muscle pull will usually settle with rest for three to five days.

Pain on the outside of the thigh can be due to inflammation in a bursa (a sac filled with fluid whose purpose is to protect the muscle from irritation from protruding bone). Irritation to the sac causes inflammation and an increase in the fluid, which in turn causes pain. Mild symptoms may settle even with running, but if symptoms are severe then rest is required. Women are more likely to develop hip pain because of the different angle that the hip bone joins onto the pelvis. Pregnancy often makes it worse. Prolonged downhill running is a potent trigger for hip pain, as is prolonged running on a camber.

Pulled hamstring muscles are common in runners and pain usually develops in the back of the thigh during or shortly after a run, usually with a particular area that is painful to touch. It may be severe enough to stop a run. Injury is most common when muscles are fatigued, during long or hard runs. Overstretching may also cause injury (the sprint for the line). If the hamstrings are weak compared to the quads at the front or are very tight (common), this increases the risk of injury. Strength and conditioning training to balance up the muscles is helpful in preventing problems and during recovery. Chronic hamstring problems can develop if minor issues are not adequately addressed.

Pain in the backside, which can radiate into the back of the thigh can be due to the piriformis syndrome. This is thought to be due to rubbing of the piriformis muscle on the nearby sciatic nerve, so the pain is similar to sciatica. Hill running and long strides are potential triggers, but sitting for long periods can also be a trigger. Specific exercises designed to stretch piriformis and the related muscle groups will help. Using a hard ball to massage the gluteal area and foam rollers are helpful.

Low back pain

The causes of low back pain are extremely complex. Sitting for long periods is the most common cause. Unequal leg length (surprisingly common), hard runs, especially on uneven ground and weak core muscles all contribute. All runners should do exercises to strengthen core muscles as part of their strength and conditioning training. Using a foam roller on the lower back can be helpful.

RUNNING-RELATED ILLNESS

Other than injuries, there are a range of more 'medical' problems attributable to running. Many of these have been covered in other sections of this book and are preventable.

Dental damage

This is not strictly a medical problem, but chronic consumption of sugary drinks and gels during runs/races will have a negative effect on the enamel of the teeth. If you can, rinse your mouth with water or sugar-free electrolyte solution after gels/sweets and brush your teeth regularly after runs.

March haemoglobinuria

This is caused by the breakdown of the red blood cells as they pass through the capillaries in the soles of the feet, due to the repeated impact. It is rare now that footwear has improved. Urine will become red-brown from the breakdown of haemoglobin released from the damaged red cells and loss of the iron-containing pigment through the kidneys. It can be difficult to distinguish from myoglobinuria.

Rhabdomyolysis and myoglobinuria

Myoglobinuria is when the pigment from myoglobin (similar to haemoglobin) is released into the circulation from damaged muscle cells. This is passed out in the urine colouring it red-brown (like cola). This is not uncommon in ultra-endurance events. Much more serious is rhabdomyolysis, where there is massive breakdown of muscle cells, with large amounts of myoglobin released into the circulation along with muscle enzymes. This can lead to serious damage to the kidneys and muscles. Severe muscle pain is usually present and the affected muscles will be very tender.

Distinguishing between haemoglobinuria, myoglobinuria and rhabdomyolysis is difficult and requires medical input urgently.

Heart problems

The development of acute chest pain, especially if radiating to the neck or into the back or arms is a possible indicator of a heart attack. The development of a very high pulse rate (inappropriate to effort) or an irregular heartbeat is also a sign to stop running immediately and seek help. Consumption of excessive amounts of caffeine before or during runs/races may contribute to an unusually fast heart rate. Alcohol is also a potential trigger for a fast and irregular heart rate and exercise may make this effect worse.

'The development of acute chest pain, especially if radiating to the neck or into the back or arms is a possible indicator of a heart attack'

Increased susceptibility to infection

There is lots of evidence that hard exercise increases the risk of minor infections for a short period afterwards, due to the impact of stress hormones on the immune cells. This effect becomes much more noticeable for endurance events, where the increased susceptibility lasts for several days.

Fatigue

Fatigue and tiredness are different. Tiredness is what you feel after a long/hard run. You will sleep better and wake the next day refreshed. On the other hand, fatigue is more draining, disturbs sleep and is not improved by sleep. It may be persistent. Fatigue is a symptom, not a diagnosis in its own right.

The initial response to persisting fatigue is to reduce/stop exercising and see whether there is an improvement. Check that diet is adequate, with enough calories, protein and fat. If there is no obvious cause, a visit to the doctor is required to undertake basic tests to rule out underlying or contributory medical conditions.

CAUSES OF FATIGUE	TYPICAL SIGNS OF FATIGUE INCLUDE
• Overtraining • Inadequate nutrition (RED-S – *see* nutrition section) • Vitamin and mineral deficiency (especially iron) • Post-infective fatigue (including long COVID) • Undiagnosed medical conditions (such as Coeliac disease, diabetes, Addison's disease or thyroid disease) • Chronic fatigue syndrome (ME)	• Disturbed, unrefreshing sleep • Headaches, dizziness, disturbed vision • Poor co-ordination • Reduction in performance (strength, endurance, speed): unexplained under-performance • Raised resting pulse rate (unless fatigue due to an underactive thyroid) • Reduced appetite • Poor concentration, attention span and memory • Reduced motivation

Short-term fatigue needs to be distinguished from long-term fatigue.

There is no quick fix unless an underlying medical condition or nutritional problem is identified. Once persistent fatigue has developed, you will rapidly slide down the greasy pole of fitness and will have to rest, then restart training again from scratch. Fitness starts reducing as soon as you stop exercising, with a noticeable deterioration within two weeks. Therefore, even when you start feeling better, you have to go back to the beginning and build up slowly again. The biggest mistake that runners make is trying to restart at the same level as they were at when the fatigue started or to build too quickly: this just makes the fatigue worse again. It can take up to a year to fully recover. It is worth discussing your training programme with an experienced coach in this setting, especially if the conclusion is that over-training/racing is to blame.

RUNNING AND PRE-EXISTING MEDICAL CONDITIONS

This section is for guidance only. The bottom line for all pre-existing medical conditions is that before starting running, you should check with your GP or other medical adviser about your exercise plans. However, there are very few absolute objections to exercise.

Anorexia and bulimia

There is a close link between eating disorders and running. Running, or other forms of strenuous exercise, are frequently used by people with eating disorders as part of their body image control. This seems to be more typical of those who run longer distances and there is an overlap with relative energy deficiency in sport (RED-S) syndrome (discussed in 'Nutrition', Chapter 4). Running in this setting is part of the need to have absolute control. Running with an eating disorder is dangerous and can lead to worsening health.

'Running with an eating disorder is dangerous and can lead to worsening health'

Chronic arthritic conditions

While there is no absolute contraindication to running in people with arthritis, and no evidence that running causes arthritis, those with established arthritis of lower limb and foot joints are likely to have more pain. People with arthritis are more likely to have developed gait abnormalities over time, as a way of protecting sore joints and these may cause problems for runners. Gait analysis may be helpful. As well as discussion with medical advisers, it is important to get good advice about appropriate footwear. Care needs to be taken when running if you are taking anti-inflammatory tablets for arthritis, as side effects in the bowel and kidneys are more likely, especially in hot weather or if you become dehydrated.

Heart disease

Heart disease, provided it has been properly investigated and treated, is not a bar to sensible exercise, including running, and most cardiac rehabilitation programmes aim to get participants fitter than they were before. Once immediate treatment has been given to open blood vessels, the patient will be up and encouraged to start exercising the next day. Heart attack victims will now usually be offered an exercise programme supervised by a cardiac rehabilitation physiotherapist. Once this is completed, exercise should continue, with appropriate medical guidance. As indicated in the introduction, a family history of early sudden death is a clear indication for further investigation before starting a strenuous exercise programme.

Lung disease

Lung disease does not prevent exercise; indeed, exercise improves all forms of lung disease. For those with asthma, the start of each run may be a struggle, especially in cold weather, so preventive use of bronchodilators before starting is wise (salbutamol or equivalent). For elite runners who are likely to be drug tested, specialist advice on asthma management from a doctor familiar with doping rules is required and therapeutic exemptions may be necessary.

Other chronic medical conditions

It is not possible to give comprehensive advice on running with every chronic health condition, but the basic rule is that unless running is physically impossible then it is likely that running in a way that is tailored to the condition is probably beneficial. Goals need to be adjusted appropriately. Exercise/running will provide mental health benefits and may help with chronic pain. Talk to professionals. For a condition such as diabetes, make sure that you learn how to manage your blood sugar during exercise and make sure you always have some glucose with you.

If you have a neurological condition which affects balance and co-ordination, then using running poles may provide additional security but select terrain carefully. Make sure that activity is carefully planned and appropriate. Try to find someone to go with you while you build up confidence. If the legs are affected, consider exercising using lightweight wheelchairs or hand-propelled trikes. Make sure that appropriate emergency information (contact numbers for family or friends, details of medical condition and medication) is stored on your phone, so it can be accessed via the emergency button on most phones and/or have a Medic-Alert bracelet.

Above all, be proud and positive about your decision to run/exercise. Dealing with chronic illness is about taking control of your life again and not allowing yourself to be defined by your illness.

FURTHER READING

First aid

Duff J. & Anderson R. *Pocket First Aid and Wilderness Medicine.* Cicerone, 3rd edition 2017, reprinted 2019.

This is an essential guide to first aid out in the mountains/wilderness. It is not a substitute for attending a practical first aid course.

Wills K. *Outdoor First Aid.* Pesda Press, 2013.

A good introduction to outdoor first aid and well illustrated. I would say essential reading for all trail, fell and mountain runners, but again not a substitute for proper practical training.

Navigation, map reading and compass skills

Hawkins P. *Map and Compass: A comprehensive guide to navigation.* Cicerone, 2nd edition 2013, reprinted 2019.

This will teach you the basics of navigation and compass use (plus proper use of GPS devices). Essential if you plan to run in remote areas or are taking part in running events that require navigation (such as the Original Mountain Marathon). Practical training may be advised as well.

Science of running

Askwith R. *The Race Against Time: Adventures in late-life running.* Yellow Jersey Press, 2023

This book looks at some of the science of running performance in the older population and has interviews with some older runners who have achieved incredible feats. It should inspire older people to get running and keep running.

Blagrove R.C. & Hayes P.R. (Eds) *The Science and Practice of Middle and Long Distance Running.* Routledge, 2021.

For those of you interested in all aspects of the science of running, this book is a mine of useful information.

Michaud T. *Injury-free Running.* Lotus Publishing, 2nd edition 2021.

This is quite a dense review of the complex biomechanics of running and their role in injury. It also covers the treatment of runners' injuries. This book is frequently referred to as the key reference work on running biomechanics, but it will be hard going for the average recreational runner. More useful to elite runners, coaches and physical therapists.

Napier C. *Science of Running: Analyse your technique, prevent injury and revolutionise your training.* Dorling Kindersley, 2020.

This is a beautifully illustrated and understandable guide to how humans run. It also covers training, strength and conditioning exercises and includes sample training plans up to marathon level. Common runners' injuries are covered.

Trail and off-road running

Koerner H. & Chase A.W. *Hal Koerner's Field Guide to Ultrarunning: Training for an ultramarathon from 50k to 100 miles and beyond.* Velo Press, 2014.

This is a valuable resource for those who want to move into ultrarunning.

Maxted C. *The Ultimate Trail Running Handbook.* Bloomsbury Sport, 2021.

Claire Maxted was the co-founder and editor of *Trail Running* magazine. This is a nicely put-together summary of how to get into trail running both short and long distance, exercises, training, gear, nutrition and hydration, with lots of illustrations. Recommended reading for beginners venturing off-road for the first time.

Rowell S. & Dodds W. *Trail and Mountain Running.* Crowood Press, 2013.

The authors are both very experienced trail and mountain runners. Wendy Dodds is also a sports physician. The book is full of valuable insights from two people who have 'been there and done that' very successfully. Full of excellent practical advice, especially for those moving on to more adventurous events.

Running injuries

Galloway J. & Hannaford D. *Running Injuries: Treatment and prevention.* Meyer & Meyer Sport, 2010.

This is a comprehensive guide to running injuries and their treatment and prevention and covers everything that might happen to a runner! This is a guide and not a substitute for appropriate professional input.

Metzl J.D. & Zimmerman M. *The Athlete's Book of Home Remedies.* Rodale Press, 2012.

This is a great straightforward guide to common injuries. It explains the symptoms, how the injury is caused, basic home treatment and preventative exercises. It makes it clear when professional help should be sought.

Running and training

Barrett S. *The HIIT Bible.* Bloomsbury, 2017.

A good explanation of HIIT, together with a useful range of exercises, some of which will require equipment.

Bateman K. & Jones H. *Older Yet Faster: The secret to running fast and injury free.* Older Yet Faster Publications, 3rd edition 2020.

This book covers running style, biomechanics and exercises (there are online videos too). The authors are very much in favour of flat (zero-drop) running shoes with thin midsoles. If you are having repeated injuries, this book is worth a look. I am not convinced however that their approach will necessarily suit everyone.

Dicharry J. *Running Rewired: Reinvent your run for stability, strength and speed.* Velo Press, 2017.

This book focuses on exercises to improve strength and conditioning for runners.

Driver J. *HIIT: High intensity interval training explained.* 2012.

An explanation of the principles of HIIT and how to implement a HIIT programme.

Felstead C. *Yoga for Runners.* Human Kinetics, 2nd Edition 2021.

This is a guide to building yoga stretches into your running training. It is an excellent and well-illustrated guide and highly recommended.

Fitzgerald M. *80/20 Running.* New American Library (Penguin), 2014.

This looks at the concept that doing 80 percent of your training at a slower pace and 20 percent at a faster pace gives better results. This is the approach the Kenyans use. It includes training plans. This works best for those doing a lot of miles per week.

Flanders L.J. *Cell Workout.* Hodder & Stoughton, 2016.

The author developed the ideas for this excellent book while a prisoner in Pentonville, with limited access to gym facilities. He studied to become a personal trainer while in prison and found that unsurprisingly there were no books on how to work out in small spaces with no equipment. This book is the result of his efforts to fill the gap, which he completed after release from prison, with support from the Princes' Trust.

Geissbuhler A. *The Ultimate Guide to HIIT: High intensity interval training.* Thunder Bay Press, 2019.

A profusely illustrated book of HIIT exercises, explaining how each exercise helps. Many of the exercises do require access to equipment.

Grantham N. *The Strength and Conditioning Bible.* Bloomsbury, 2015.

Nick Grantham is an S&C coach who has worked with Olympic athletes and premier league football clubs. It provides the background to S&C training and details of exercise programmes, with copious illustrations. Recommended.

Hilditch G. *Marathon and Half Marathon: A training guide.* Crowood Press, 2nd edition 2014.

A useful guide with training plans and nutritional advice to get you fit to run a marathon.

Karp J.R. *Running Periodization: Training theories to run faster.* Coaches Choice, 2021.

This is the best book explaining periodisation of training in an understandable format. It discusses it from the perspective of an athlete who is struggling to progress. Sample training programmes are included. It is an American publication that does not appear to be marketed in the UK, but you can order it through Amazon. Thoroughly recommended.

Magill P., Schwartz T. & Breyer M. *Build your running body.* Souvenir Press 2015.

A wonderful encyclopedia of everything you could ever need to know about how to run. Profusely illustrated

Murphy S. *Run Your Best Marathon: Your trusted guide to training and racing better.* Bloomsbury Sport, 2022.

Sam Murphy is a regular contributor to *Runner's World* and is a coach and fitness instructor. This is a very up-to-date book with lots of very useful advice. It covers a lot of the science behind running well and incorporates training programmes. Worth a read.

Shepherd J. *Strength Training for Runners.* Bloomsbury, 2013.

This is a very useful book which explains the basic principles of strength exercises for runners, with illustrations and explanations of key exercises. The science behind strength training is also discussed in an understandable format. Recommended.

Yamauchi M. *Marathon Wisdom: An elite athlete's insights on running and life.* Meyer & Meyer Sport, 2022.

This book is written by Mara Yamauchi, an internationally successful marathon runner, now retired and working as a running coach. It is a reflection on what she learned about preparing for and running marathons and most of the lessons that she learned, often the hard way, are entirely applicable to recreational runners.

Magazines

Runner's World: https://www.hearstmagazines.co.uk/runners-world-magazine-subscription

Runner's World also has a US version and both have valuable websites with excellent articles for runners.

Ultrarunner: https://www.ultrarunnermagazine.co.uk

Ultra magazine: https://www.ultra-magazine.com

Sadly, *Trail Running*, the UK magazine for trail runners, ceased publication at the end of 2022 (being subsumed into *Trail* magazine, which is almost exclusively devoted to hiking). There is still a website. There are other trail running magazines for other countries.

RESOURCES

Useful websites

Countryside Code
https://assets.publishing.service.gov.uk/
government/uploads/system/uploads/
attachment_data/file/1014038/countryside-
code-summary.pdf

Race pace calculators
https://www.calculator.net/pace-calculator.
html
https://www.ukresults.net/misc/predictor.html

MHR calculator
https://www.topendsports.com/fitness/
karvonen-formula-calculator.htm

Training plans and exercises
https://www.greatrun.org/train-and-prepare/
training-plans/
https://www.mcmillanrunning.com
https://www.runnersworld.com/training/
g23341982/best-bodyweight-exercises/
https://www.runnersworld.com/uk/
training-plans/
https://www.womensrunning.com/training/
cross-training/yoga-poses-runners-avoid/
https://www.yogaforrunners.com

Windchill calculator
https://www.weather.gov/epz/wxcalc_
windchill

Templates; Route cards/running logs
https://www.silvanavigationschool.com/prod-
uct-category/freebies/:
https://www.vertex42.com/ExcelTemplates/
running-log.html

Resources for hill runners
https://www.ukclimbing.com/articles/skills/
series/running/walk_before_you_run_-_
winter_skills_for_hill_runners-13243

Resources for health
https://www.nhs.uk/live-well/healthy-weight/
bmi-calculator/
https://runnersconnect.net/calories/
https://www.runsociety.com/health-injuries/
nipple-tape-how-to-prevent-nipple-
chafing-for-long-distance-runners/

Resources for events and challenges
https://ace-races.co.uk
https://www.canix.co.uk
https://www.endurancelife.com/
trail-ultra-marathons
https://www.fellrunner.org.uk
https://www.hardmoors110.org.uk
https://www.lakelandtrails.org
https://www.parkrun.org.uk
https://www.raceatyourpace.co.uk
https://runnation.co.uk
https://www.runthings.co.uk
https://www.spartanrace.uk/en
https://www.theconqueror.events
https://toughmudder.co.uk
https://www.thresholdtrailseries.com
https://www.ultrachallenge.com

Resources for clothing and equipment
https://www.bridgedale.com
https://harrierrunfree.co.uk
https://icegripper.co.uk/products/icespike
https://www.irunfar.com/best-winter-running-
traction-devices
https://www.kisi.co.uk/canicross-gear

https://www.parkrun.org.uk/shop/
https://rerunclothing.org
https://ruffwear.co.uk/
www.trailrunning.co.uk
https://www.yaktrax.co.uk

Running groups
https://www.blacktrailrunners.run
www.therunninggranny.co.uk
https://www.runthings.co.uk
https://www.thisgirlcan.co.uk/activities/running/
https://www.veganrunners.org.uk

Resources for disabled athletes
www.englandathletics.org/findaguide
https://www.scope.org.uk/advice-and-support/disability-sport/

Resources for tracking apps
https://www.mapmyrun.com
https://www.plotaroute.com/
https://www.strava.com/features

Resources for recipes
https://www.runnersworld.com/uk/nutrition/recipes/g26530519/best-homemade-energy-bars/
https://www.runnersworld.com/uk/nutrition/recipes/a774179/diy-sports-drink/
https://www.trailrunnermag.com/nutrition/race-day-nutrition-nutrition/3-diy-energy-bars-for-your-next-run/)

Resources for specialist food and drinks
https://highfive.co.uk/collections/all-products/
https://www.mountainfuel.co.uk
https://www.precisionhydration.com
https://www.scienceinsport.com/shop-sis/all-products
https://www.tailwindnutrition.co.uk

ACKNOWLEDGEMENTS

This book is the sum of what I have learned over half a lifetime of running and training and over that time I have met innumerable people, all of whom have influenced my thinking in big or small ways. I am particularly grateful to my current run training group, led by Alun 'Woody' Woodward and including Iain Fenwick, Karen Singleton, Sarah Hamilton, Sarah Bell, Marcella Shone and Rosie Carr, all of whom have contributed their experiences via pre- and post-run chats and some have very kindly reviewed and commented on the manuscript. Woody and his partner Jo Shallcross have been a huge influence on me, from when they first met me to consider run retraining, to advice and coaching on all aspects of endurance running and strength and conditioning training. Both kindly volunteered to be photographed. Jo runs The Barn Fitness and was kind enough to supervise me while I was working for my fitness instructor qualification.

Others over the years who have been particularly helpful are Gary Nash, James Kent and Derek Wilson from the Outdoor Fitness Company. I am also grateful to my running colleagues from Tyndale Harriers, when I was younger and faster. I have also appreciated the advice and help over many years from my local running stores (Start Fitness, Northern Runner, both Newcastle, Chivers Sports in Carlisle and Pete Bland Sports in Kendal). Over the years of competing, it has been a pleasure dealing with Lakeland Trails, who run fabulous trail events in the Lake District and Richard Hunter of Run Nation, who started out with a run at Wallington House in Northumberland but now has running events all over the country. Thank you everyone.

I am very grateful to Run Nation (Richard Hunter) and Lakeland Trails (Phil Blaylock and photographers James Kirby, Graham Millington and Carlos Reina) for permission to reproduce some of their event photographs featuring the author.

I am extremely grateful to The Crowood Press for their unstinting help and support in the preparation of this book.

Finally, I must thank my long-suffering wife Sally, who not only puts up with me spending large amounts of time running but also large amounts of time writing books, including this one. She describes herself as a running widow!

INDEX